Religion in Human Culture

The Hindu Tradition

WORLD RELIGIONS CURRICULUM DEVELOPMENT CENTER
MINNEAPOLIS, MINNESOTA

Project Co-Directors: Lee Smith and Wes Bodin
Project Assistants: Joan Voigt and Pat Noyes

Argus Communications
Niles, Illinois 60648

Photo Credits

Cover Photos
Toby Mollenaar/ALPHA PHOTO ASSOCIATES lower right
CYR COLOR PHOTO AGENCY middle right
Jean-Claude LeJeune lower middle
Bernard Pierre Wolff/MAGNUM PHOTOS top
R. Khullar/VAN CLEVE PHOTOGRAPHY lower left

Page Photos
- 3 R. Khullar/BRUCE COLEMAN INC.
- 6 D. Pike/BRUCE COLEMAN INC.
- 10 Harry Miller/SHOSTAL ASSOCIATES
- 15 D. M. Knipe
- 18 SHOSTAL ASSOCIATES
- 22 C. B. Naik/SHOSTAL ASSOCIATES
- 23 SHOSTAL ASSOCIATES
- 25 H. D. Shourie/SHOSTAL ASSOCIATES
- 26 SHOSTAL ASSOCIATES upper left, upper right
  R. Khullar/VAN CLEVE PHOTOGRAPHY lower left
  L. L. T. Rhodes/VAN CLEVE PHOTOGRAPHY lower right
- 30 Keith Gunnar/BRUCE COLEMAN INC.
- 35/39 B. Bhansali/SHOSTAL ASSOCIATES
- 42 M. Matherson/SHOSTAL ASSOCIATES
- 51/54/55 B. Bhansali/SHOSTAL ASSOCIATES
- 57 D. M. Knipe
- 58 SHOSTAL ASSOCIATES
- 63 M. P. Kahl/BRUCE COLEMAN INC.
- 66 K. Kummels/SHOSTAL ASSOCIATES
- 71 B. Bhansali/SHOSTAL ASSOCIATES
- 75 D. M. Knipe
- 78 SHOSTAL ASSOCIATES
- 83/87 B. Kapur/SHOSTAL ASSOCIATES
- 90 SHOSTAL ASSOCIATES
- 91 B. Bhansali/SHOSTAL ASSOCIATES

Acknowledgments

Excerpts from Wm. Theodore de Bary et al. (eds.): *Sources of Indian Tradition,* New York: Columbia University Press, 1958, pp. 284-85, 298, 286-87, 289, by permission of the publisher.

Excerpts from *The Hindu Tradition,* edited by Ainslie T. Embree. Copyright © 1966 by Random House, Inc. Reprinted by permission of the publisher.

Excerpt from *The Wheel of Life* by Donald J. Johnson and Jean E. Johnson. Copyright © 1974 by Praeger Publishers. Reprinted by permission of Praeger Publishers, a division of Holt, Rinehart and Winston.

Excerpt from *India: A World in Transition,* Fourth Edition by Beatrice Pitney Lamb. Copyright © 1963, 1966, 1968, and 1975 by Beatrice Pitney Lamb. Reprinted by permission of Praeger Publishers, a division of Holt, Rinehart and Winston.

Excerpts from Barbara Stoler Miller (trans.): *Bhartrihari: Poems,* New York: Columbia University Press, 1967, by permission of the publishers.

Excerpt from *The Religion of the Hindus—Interpreted by Hindus,* edited by Kenneth W. Morgan. Copyright 1953 The Ronald Press Company, New York. Reprinted by permission.

Excerpt from *Cradle Tales of Hinduism* by Sister Nivedita. Calcutta: Advaita Ashrama, 1968. Reprinted with permission.

Excerpt from *The Great Religions By Which Men Live* by Floyd H. Ross and Tynette Hills. Copyright © 1954, 1956 by Beacon Press. Reprinted by permission of Beacon Press.

Excerpt adapted from pp. 16-29 in *The Religions of Man* (hardbound edition) by Huston Smith. Copyright © 1958 by Huston Smith. Reprinted by permission of Harper & Row, Publishers, Inc.

Excerpts from *The Bhagavad Gita.* A New Verse Translation by Ann Stanford. © 1970 by Herder & Herder, Inc. Used by permission of the publisher, The Seabury Press, New York.

Excerpt adapted from pp. 151-158 in *Like a Great River: An Introduction to Hinduism* by Herbert Stroup. Copyright © 1972 by Herbert Stroup. Reprinted by permission of Harper & Row, Publishers, Inc.

Religion in Human Culture is a project of St. Louis Park Independent School District #283, Title III/IV (Part C), ESEA, and the Northwest Area Foundation. The opinions and other contents of this book do not necessarily reflect the position or policy of the State of Minnesota, the U.S. Government, St. Louis Park ISD #283, or the Northwest Area Foundation, and no official endorsement should be inferred.

Designed by Gene Tarpey

© Copyright Argus Communications 1978.

All rights reserved. No portion of this book may be reproduced, stored in a retrieval system, or transmitted in any form by any means—electronic, mechanical, photocopying, recording or otherwise—without prior permission of the copyright owner.

Printed in the United States of America.

Argus Communications
7440 Natchez Avenue
Niles, Illinois 60648

International Standard Book Number
0-89505-005-6

Library of Congress Number
78-53805

0 9 8 7 6 5 4 3 2 1

Contents

NOTE TO THE READER   V

1. Historical Introduction to Hinduism   *Paul J. Will*   1
2. Basic Concepts of Hinduism   *Donald J. Johnson and Jean E. Johnson*   7
3. Gods and Goddesses Among the Hindus, Past and Present   *Beatrice Pitney Lamb*   19
4. How Many Gods?   29
5. The Goals of Hindu Life   *Huston Smith*   31
6. Caste   *Herbert Stroup*   49
7. The Stages of Life   *Floyd H. Ross and Tynette Hills*   59
8. The Role of Women in Hinduism   *Kenneth W. Morgan*   65
9. The Paths   *Ainslie T. Embree*   67
10. Stories, Festivals, and Devotion   *Paul Younger and Susanna Oommen Younger*   81

GLOSSARY   93

Note to the Reader

This book is a collection of readings which have been taken from a variety of sources. It is not to be considered or used as a conventional textbook; rather, the readings are intended as a source of data or information on various practices and concepts found in the Hindu tradition. A study and analysis of this data should increase your understanding not only of Hinduism but of the people who practice this tradition.

    The study of Hinduism presents special problems. The Hindu tradition is extremely diverse and therefore cannot be known in its entirety. It has cultural qualities that are almost impossible to study with Western methods of scholarship because direct parallels do not exist in Western cultures. The result is that Westerners run a high risk of getting a distorted picture of Hinduism. The difficulty in this book is compounded by the fact that the writings or scriptures contain the Sanskrit names of the many gods and heroes of the religion. It is suggested that you avoid getting "hung up" on these technicalities and try instead to stay in touch with the ideas and concepts and to develop a "feel" for Hinduism. It should also be noted that the readings contain inconsistencies in organization and in spelling. These inconsistencies result from the fact that the readings are from a variety of sources and different authors organize the same material in different ways and incorporate different translations of the Sanskrit in their writings.

To facilitate your reading, a glossary of several terms relevant to Hinduism is provided at the back of this book. As you encounter words you are unfamiliar with, refer to the glossary for their definitions.

READING 1
Historical Introduction to Hinduism
PAUL J. WILL

Religion is often thought of as an institution or system that can be analyzed. In reality, for many people it is a way of life that is in a constant state of change. Religion is complex and diverse. Nowhere is this clearer than with Hinduism, which is probably the oldest religious tradition in the world. Hinduism has survived because of its ability to adjust to new historical forces. Hindus claim their religion has no origin or beginning and is eternal.

Hinduism is like an encyclopedia of religion. Almost every form of religious expression and belief is represented. Yet it lacks many of the elements commonly felt to be part of religion: a historical founder, a highly organized priesthood, and a required creed of beliefs. The religion known as Hinduism can be compared to an onion. It consists basically of layers. The Hindu tradition is made up of the contributions of many cultures and people. Over the centuries, new ideas and practices were absorbed and modified. Today, while some of these are lost, there is still much continuity with the past.

Numerous cultures have contributed to Hinduism. Before the first major civilization in South Asia, there was a basic peasant culture which showed respect toward animals and plants. Later, the Indus Valley civilization (2300–1700 B.C.) in northwestern India apparently introduced a mother goddess cult that stressed the feminine element. Purification with water was probably an important ritual in this religion. Its effect is still seen in the bathing at the temple tank. Clear examples of animal and sexual worship are also found in the remains of this culture.

With the arrival of the Aryan people in India, the Vedic Period (1400–500 B.C.) began. While many aspects of Vedic religion have disappeared or changed, there are still some left in Hinduism. Most of the gods worshipped by the Aryans are of little importance today. The chief ritual of sacrifice has been replaced by other methods of religious practice. The Vedic rites of passage, however, have been kept in modified form to the present. These rituals are performed at important periods of change or "passage" in one's life, such as being born, becoming an adult, getting married, and facing death. The Indian social class system began in this period. As time went on, a rigid caste system developed. It helped Indian society and Hinduism survive a number of foreign invasions and internal problems. The caste system resulted in a conservative society but one that tolerated differences. Each member of society had his own *dharma* (duty) to follow.[1]

The greatest contribution of the Aryan people was a set of sacred writings that laid the foundation for the Hindu world view. The *Vedas,* from the word *veda* meaning "knowledge," form the supreme authority for Hindus. This Vedic literature is considered *shruti,* "that which is heard," or eternal. All Hindus accept it as authoritative. It includes both hymns and later commentaries. The most important section, called the *Upanishads,* represented a new development in Vedic religion. To a large extent, this section was a reaction to a religion filled with ritual and controlled by priests. The *Upanishads* tried to deal with questions about the meaning of life and the nature of the universe.

The *Upanishads* discuss the relation between Brahman (the ultimate reality or Universal Self) and the *atman* (inner self). Most Hindus accept the idea of a relationship between *atman* and Brahman but disagree over the nature of this relationship. However, the Hindu tradition has always allowed a variety of religious interpretations. New ideas such as *samsara* (reincarnation, or being born again and again in different forms) and *karma* (the effect that thoughts, words, and deeds have on a person's

---

[1] The caste system is treated in more detail in a later reading.

Hindus bathe in the Ganges River at Hardwar ("Vishnu's Gate"). A stone believed to contain Vishnu's footprint is part of the upper wall of the bathing steps, or ghat.

past, present, and future) were introduced. These concepts gradually gained acceptance in Hindu society.

There were other reactions to the ritualistic Vedic religion in the period from 600 to 200 B.C. Two separate religions which exist today, Buddhism and Jainism, originated in India at this time. As they developed, the Vedic religion continued changing. Present-day Hinduism is really the merging of many of these diverse religious ideas and practices. Nevertheless, ever since the writing of the *Upanishads,* the generally accepted goal of Hindus is to gain release from the cycle of reincarnation and to achieve realization of or unity with Brahman, the ultimate reality.

Various methods to accomplish this end were developed. They include ascetic or self-denying practices, meditative and yogic exercises, devotional worship, ethical behavior, and ritual acts. Yoga (spiritual discipline) and asceticism have been present since the very beginning of Hindu religion. The *Bhagavad-Gita* (Song of the Blessed Lord) was written in an attempt to synthesize these different methods. It reconciled the ascetic and yogic tradition with the priestly religion and the followers of ritual. Caste duties were made religious duties, thus strengthening the ties between society and religion.

Most importantly, the *Gita* endorsed *bhakti* (devotionalism) as the best means to salvation. Its stress on devotion toward a personalized deity, in this case Krishna, was a new emphasis in Hinduism. Salvation for many Hindus is seen in terms of faith and devotion toward a particular god or goddess, who is a manifestation of the ultimate. Most Hindus are not members of distinct sects or religious groups. However, there are numerous devotees of particular deities, the most important being Shiva, Vishnu, and their Shaktis (Powers). The appeal of *bhakti* lies in the promise of salvation for the devotee. The worship of a personal deity became a major theme in the Medieval or Middle Period (200 B.C.–A.D. 1800). During this period different schools of philosophy and religious interpretation developed.

Generally, each Hindu will combine different elements from the religious tradition in forming his own personal religious position. Since most Hindus live in villages, they have little familiarity with the scriptural heritage. Instead, pilgrimages, festivals, temple worship, domestic rituals, and ethical actions are the focus of their religion. Their understanding of Hinduism may come through religious epics and stories like the *Mahabharata,* which includes the *Gita,* and the *Ramayana.* These epics are part of the *smriti* literature, "that which is remembered." They are considered secondary to the *shruti* Vedic literature, but for many people the *smriti* literature is the main source of religious values.

An important influence on Hinduism came with the introduction of Islam into India. Many Muslim ideas influenced Hindu thought, especially the *bhakti* tradition. Sikhism, a religion that drew on both Hindu and Muslim religious ideas, developed in the late 1400s. After 1800 Hindu beliefs were challenged by new ideas from the West. Many criticisms were made of Hindu practices. Once again Hinduism adapted to meet new conditions. The result was a revitalized and reformed religion.

Hinduism remains a great world religion with over 500,000,000 followers. It has changed and adapted over the years. Hinduism's close links to Indian society and culture helped it to survive. It is like a pot of stew in which new ingredients are added. Each of the new religious ideas and practices becomes part of the religion but still can be identified as a distinctive element. Although Hindus traditionally have not sought converts, new groups like the Hare Krishna movement are actively seeking followers. They are carrying Hindu ideas outside of South Asia where most Hindus live. Historically there have been migrations of Hindus to Southeast Asia, Africa, and the Caribbean. In recent times, there have been many Hindus who have moved to England and North America. The twentieth century finds Hindus continuing to follow and modify a tradition composed of five thousand years of religious experience.

A woman hangs a garland on her home shrine.

READING 2
Basic Concepts of Hinduism*
DONALD J. JOHNSON and JEAN E. JOHNSON

Most Hindus accept the concept of Brahman-atman as the explanation about the nature of the universe and their own identity. However, they do not agree about the nature of Brahman and its relationship to atman. Some see Brahman as an impersonal absolute and describe it as the ultimate reality, the "One." Ultimately, everything is Brahman, yet it cannot be described in human terms. Others view Brahman as a personal deity or god with which one can communicate. Some Hindus view the ultimate goal as complete absorption of the atman (inner self) with Brahman (Universal Self) with a corresponding loss of individuality. Others believe that one comes to know and commune intimately with Brahman. But there is still a distinction between Brahman and atman.

Hindus think that there are numerous opportunities to achieve their goal through the cycle of reincarnation, or transmigration (samsara). A person's karma (thoughts, words, and actions) affects his or her reincarnation pattern. By following one's dharma (duty), one can accumulate good karmic effects. Thus the idea of karma is not fatalistic, for one can shape the future through present actions. At death what passes from one

---

*From Donald J. Johnson and Jean E. Johnson, eds., *The Wheel of Life,* vol. 1 of *Through Indian Eyes* (New York: Praeger Publishers, 1974), pp. 128–41.

existence to another is the *atman* and the *karma* that has not had its effect. *Moksha (liberation from reincarnation) comes when no new* karma *is produced and the old* karma *is exhausted. Then the true nature of the universe is known, and according to some, what was observed as real is seen to be only passingly real* (maya).

These concepts are developed in the following reading. One needs to remember that Hindus tolerate a wide variety of interpretations and thus no explanation of Hindu religious concepts is final. English translations for Sanskrit terms are often not precise and only point further to this diversity. Note also that the concept of Brahman is referred to as God in this reading.

AS YOU SOW, SO SHALL YOU REAP: *KARMA*

"Two days ago the marriage feast was mine,
And only yesterday I bought milch kine [milk cows]
Wherewith to start my modest home. My field
Is bright with corn, with gold my coffers yield,
I cannot die." While yet thou speakest, fool,
Dread Yama's [God of Death] step comes near. Farewell, vile soul.

Chorus: How near is death! Mercy he cannot bring.
Then, oh my heart, cease from the world, and cling
With all thy power to tender Lakshmi's King [Vishnu, the God of Preservation].

"My house is newly built, E'en now they say
The Mantras [holy verses] that have power to drive away
All evils from my home. My wife is great
With child. The day that weds my son we wait.
Life is so good, I cannot, will not, die."
Vain fool! Death's hand now shades thy glazing eye.

Chorus: How near is death! &c.[1]

Death can come at any time, as this Canarese folk song suggests. But to the Hindu death is but one point on the great span of endless time. An individual dies, but in India that is not the end of his story. All Hindus know:

To him that is born, death is sure
And for him who has died, birth is certain.
This cannot be changed.[2]

[1] Canarese folk-song, "The Nearness of Death," from Charles E. Cover, *The Folk-Songs of Southern India* (Madras: South India Saiva Siddhanta Works Publishing Society, 1959), p. 18.
[2] From Ann Stanford, trans., *The Bhagavad Gita* (New York: The Seabury Press, 1970), 2:27.

Another Hindu scripture explains:

> As the body of mortals undergoes the changes of infancy, youth and old age, even so will it be transformed, into another body hereafter; a sensible man is not mistaken about that. As a man puts on new clothes in this world, throwing aside those which he formerly wore, even so the self of man puts on new bodies which are in accordance with his acts in a former life.[3]

Although an individual may die, his life force or soul (called *atman*) never dies; it takes on a new form with each birth. *Samsara* ("rebirth") is more than a belief to the Hindu or Buddhist. It is the certainty on which all life is based. . . .

The factor that determines the form in which you will be born in your next existence is your *karma.* If you have lived a good life, you build up good *karma* and will be born into a higher station, or to a happier life. If you perform bad deeds, you build up bad *karma* and are certain to suffer in succeeding lives. Good and bad *karma* are built up over generations, the balance being passed on to future lives.

In the New Testament, Saint Matthew states, "As a man soweth, so also shall he reap." The difference between this statement and *karma* is that to St. Matthew, a man's deeds are balanced out in a single lifetime, whereas *karma* is the balancing of good and bad deeds over hundreds of lifetimes.

The Upanishads, one of the Hindu holy books, describes this process:

> Those whose conduct here [on earth] has been good will quickly attain some good birth—birth as a Brahmin [priest or seer], birth as a Kshatriya [administrator or warrior], or birth as a Vaishya [producer]. But those whose conduct here has been evil will quickly attain some evil birth—birth as a dog, birth as a pig, or birth as a *chandala* ("untouchable").[4]

Karma also helps to explain the seeming unfairness of life. Why does a child get hit by a car? Why does a young father die of cancer? Why did that housewife win the lottery ticket? Many Indians answer these kinds of questions by the law of *karma.* When they see a good man suffer, Indians might say: "It's because of some bad deed done in a previous life. Who can escape his *karma?*" Likewise, good *karma* follows a man:

[3] Louis Renon, *Hinduism* (New York: George Braziller, 1961), p. 129.
[4] Nikhilanarda, *The Upanishads* (New York: Harper and Row, 1964), p. 321.

In dark forest, amidst his foes in war,
In flood or raging flame;
In ocean depths or on precarious peaks;
Slumbering or courting dread danger
With reckless abandon;
Merits earned in former lives
Afford a man protection.[5]

Living, for the Hindu, can be seen as an attempt to build up good *karma.* But one builds good *karma* not by "doing good" or helping old ladies across the street but by doing one's duty, one's *dharma.* If you are a son, you obey your father even if it means banishment. If you are a tailor, you bring up your sons to be good tailors. Each person has a *dharma,* determined in part by his position in the family, his caste, and his age. A son obeys; a sweeper cleans the street; a wife bears children. All are human, but each must be faithful to his *dharma.*

But what if you think your *dharma* is wrong? Suppose you think doing your *dharma* will hurt others. The traditional Hindu answer is a story.

Imagine a mighty warrior about to fight in a great battle. On the eve of the conflict, he looks out at the enemy forces and there sees some of his dearest friends, his beloved uncle, his cousins, and even his *guru.* "How can I fight those whom I honor and love? Better I should die. I will not fight." With these words, he throws down his arms and sits despondently near his chariot.

This is the situation in the *Bhagavad Gita,* perhaps the best-loved Hindu sacred text. Arjuna, the brave Pandava warrior, refuses to fight against his cousins, the Kauravas. But Arjuna's charioteer is an incarnation of God, the Lord Krishna. Hearing Arjuna's words, Krishna advises the warrior:

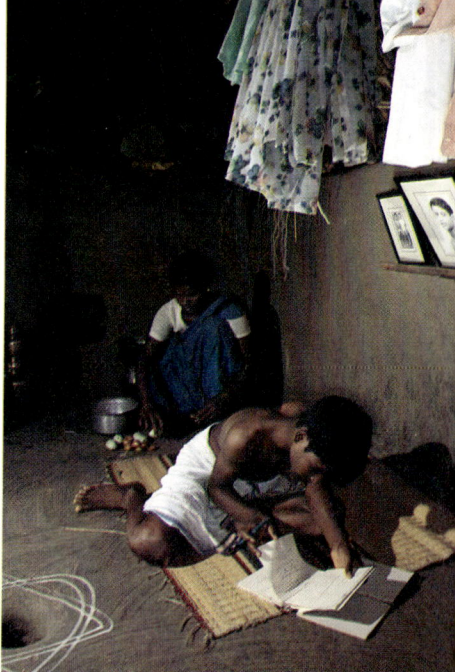

An Indian schoolboy does his homework while his mother (in the background) prepares a meal.

> You grieve for those you should not
> And yet you talk about wisdom.
> The truly taught do not mourn
> For the dead or the living.
>
> For to him that is born death is sure
> And for him who has died, birth is certain.
> This cannot be changed. Therefore,
> You should not sorrow.

[5] Barbara Stoler Miller, *Bhartrihari: Poems* (New York: Columbia University Press, 1967), p. 46.

And if you think just of your own place
You should not recoil.
For a warrior there is no better thing
Than to fight out of duty.

Here chance is offering you
A door open to heaven.
O Partha, those warriors are lucky
Who are granted such a fight.

But if you turn away from this battle
Which your own duty requires
Then, giving up duty and glory,
You will only get trouble.

People will talk of your shame
Now and in years to come.
And for one who has been honored
Disgrace is worse than death.

Those in the great chariots will be sure
That you hang back from the battle through fear
And they who once thought well of you
Will come to hold you lightly.

Those who wish you ill will talk of you
And say what had best not be said.
They will revile all that you are.
What could be worse than that?

Either killed, you shall gain heaven
Or conquering, you will enjoy the earth.
Therefore, stand up, son of Kunti
And set your mind upon battle.

Holding pleasure and pain as alike
Gain and loss, victory and defeat
Prepare yourself for the fight
Only thus will you not reap evil.

Better do your own task imperfectly
Than do another's well.
Better die in your own duty.
Another's task brings peril.[6]

Lord Krishna's advice to Arjuna is the model for *dharma* for all Hindus: Do your duty. But there is more to it than that. Think for a minute why *you* act. Why do you study for a test? Why do you tell

---

[6]Stanford, *Gita* 2:11, 27, 31–38; 3:35; pp. 14–31.

the truth? Why did you come to school this morning? Why do you obey your parents?

Now put your answers aside and consider these words Krishna says to Arjuna:

> You have a right to the work alone
> But never to its fruits.
> Let not the fruits be your motive . . .
>
> Steadfast in the Way, without attachment,
> Do your work, Victorious One.
> The same in success and misfortune.
> This evenness—that is discipline.[7]

Your business is with the deed, not with the result. Just do your duty and let the results fall where they may. A fire burns; the flame cannot be concerned about whether it cooks food or destroys lives. Rain falls alike on the "just and the unjust." Do your duty with a "holy indifference for the results." The result may be banishment or a kingdom; these facts do not affect your *dharma*.

Doing your duty with no concern for the fruits of your actions is the way to build up good *karma* and to be born into a higher life in your next incarnation. Violate your *dharma*, seek the fruits of your actions, and you carry the bad *karma* into future lifetimes. Build up enough good *karma* and you will not be born again at all. As Krishna states:

> The wise, whose minds are controlled,
> Leaving the rewards of action,
> Are released from the bounds of rebirth.[8]

ALL IS ONE: THE HINDU CONCEPT OF GOD

The final goal in life for the Hindu is not to be born into a higher station in his next life. The final goal is not to be born again at all. The ultimate result of good *karma* is that a person is reunited with God.

What is the Hindu concept of God? Is it similar to Allah of the Muslims or Yaweh of the Jews or God the Father of the Christians? In the following passage, Krishna describes the nature of God to Arjuna. Remember, Krishna is an incarnation of God, so he speaks of himself. How does this concept of God compare to your own?

[7]*Ibid.* 2:47, 48.
[8]*Ibid.* 2:51.

I am immortality and death
What is and what is not, Arjuna.

I am the source of all.
All things come forth from me.

I am the beginning and the end
And the middle of all creations
I am the knowledge of the soul.
I am the discourse of those who speak.

I am the gambling of the cheat
The sharp edge of the brilliant.
I am victory. I am effort.
I am courage to the stout-hearted.

Understanding, knowledge, non-delusion
Patience, restraint, truth, serenity,
Courage and fear, joy and sorrow,
Rising up and passing away,

Harmlessness, equanimity, content,
Austerity, open-handedness
Fame, ill-fame, however various,
These states of being arise from me alone.

And whatever is the seed of all beings
That I am, Arjuna.
No creature that moves or does not move
Could exist without me.[9]

Note that Krishna says that he and he alone is the "source of all"—of creation, destruction, fame, ill-fame, love, and hate. The single source is that invisible and subtle essence that pervades all things, which we call God. This God is all that is, and all that is not, as well. It is the ONEness of all reality. To be the ONE, it must combine all opposites within itself.

In the Judeo-Christian tradition and also in Islam, God generally stands for only good qualities, such as love, justice, truth, and peace. Another figure, usually the Devil, is the source of evil: hate, injustice, falsehood, sin, etc. In these religions, one has a choice between God, representing good, and the Devil, representing evil. You either go God's way or the Devil's. Notice the word *or*. The choice is good *or* evil, God *or* the Devil.

In the Hindu concept, however, ultimate reality is *both* rather than *either*. The ONE is both good and evil, both God and the Devil.

[9]*Ibid.* 9:19, 10:8, 32, 36, 4, 5, 39.

Destruction is as much a part of the ONE as is creation. Both exist; therefore, they exist in the ONE.

But you and I exist as well. What is our relationship to the ONE? Listen to the way in which a father explains this to his son, Svetaketu, in the *Upanishads:*

> "Place this salt in water and come to me tomorrow morning."
>
> Svetaketu did as he was commanded, and in the morning his father said to him: "Bring me the salt you put into the water last night."
>
> Svetaketu looked into the water, but could not find it, for it had dissolved.
>
> His father then said: "Taste the water from this side. How is it?"
>
> "It is salt."
>
> "Taste it from the middle. How is it?"
>
> "It is salt."
>
> "Look for the salt again and come again to me."
>
> The son did so, saying, "I cannot see the salt. I only see water."
>
> His father then said: "In the same way, O my son, you cannot see the Spirit. But in truth he is here."
>
> An invisible and subtle essence is the Spirit of the whole universe. That is Reality. That is Truth. THOU ART THAT.[10]

Christianity and Islam believe that man stands in relationship to God. He may pray to God, walk with God, perhaps even see and hear God, but he can never *be* God. In the Hindu conception of the ONE, all things *are* God, and therefore man is God too. The ONE is you, it is me, it is ALL.

Yet God is not you. That is why many Hindus, when describing God, speak in negative terms. God is not this, not that, not knowing, not unknowing. What we see and experience is not God, yet God is All.

In talking about God we are like the six blind men disputing the correct description of an elephant that none of us can see. We have mistaken what we can see, touch, smell, hear, and taste for the true and complete reality. This perception that physical phenomena are real Hindus call *maya. Maya,* from the same root as the word "magic," means illusion. It is as if the universal reality were playing tricks on us, making us believe that our bodies, this page, the mountains, and the birds are real. In Hinduism, one must go past these material forms to the one divine mystery that

---

[10] Juan Mascaro, *The Upanishads* (Baltimore: Penguin Books, 1965), pp. 117–18.

envelops and manifests itself as all the little realities. That is the one true reality. *Maya* is simply the mistaken belief that lesser things are real.

Joseph Campbell, a famous scholar of world mythologies, tells the story of a kitten before a mirror who sees what he thinks is another kitten. He stalks it, boxes with it, even rubs noses with it.

The Hindu cremation rite is the beginning of a series of rituals designed to advance the deceased to his or her next life.

Finally he peeks behind the mirror and then realizes that he has been reacting to an image. Like the kitten, you and I spend our days loving and fighting things that are ultimately illusionary, according to the theory of *maya*. Even you and I in our separate forms are illlusions, say the Hindus, for we are all part of the ONE we call God.

SEEKING REUNION WITH GOD: *MOKSHA*

Because we live in the world of *maya*, we do not know that we are God. In our daily lives we experience life as separate beings, living, dying and being born again, living, dying and again being born. At some point in his experience, after several lifetimes, or several thousand lifetimes, the Hindu grows weary of living on earth, no matter how pleasant it may be. Swami Ramakrishna, the great Hindu teacher, described the process:

> The world is like a stage, where men perform many parts under various disguises. They do not like to take off the mask, unless they have played for some time. Let them play for a while, and then they will leave off the mask of their own accord.

Most everyone is still "playing for a while," but if we are Hindus we know that the time will come when we will want to "leave off the mask." When that time does come, we are ready to seek reunion with God (*moksha*). We are ready to seek to realize the Oneness of all things and in this realization to merge with the ONE even as a drop of water joins the ocean.

To experience reunion with the ONE is the goal of the last half of life. Even if you have been a success in this world, life on the wheel of birth and rebirth is not enough.

> If wealth which yields all desire is won,
>   What then?
> If your foot stands on the head of your foes,
>   What then?
> If honored men are drawn to you by your riches' force,
>   What then?
> If man's mundane body endures for an aeon,
>   What then?[11]

---

[11] Miller, *Bhartrihari, 186, p. 137.*

When a Hindu sees that even if he were to achieve his desires he would still ask, "What then?" he is ready to give up his role as a Householder and seek God. The Laws of Manu [laws of conduct given by an ancient patriarch] give clear instructions for this action:

> When a householder sees his [skin] wrinkled and [his hair] white, and the sons of his sons, then he may resort to the forest. Abandoning all food raised by cultivation and all his belongings, he may depart into the forest, either committing his wife to his sons or accompanied by her.[12]

Many examples from the history and mythology of India hold up this idea of "going to the forest." The individual personality (the ego) disappears.

> Once upon a time, in those bright ages when India was young, there lived a great king, Bharata, and so famous was he that even now the people speak among themselves of their country as Bharata Varsha, Bharata's Land; it is only foreigners who talk of it as "India."
>
> In the days of this ruler, it was considered the right thing for every man, when he had finished educating his family—when his daughters were all married, his business affairs in order, and his sons well-established in life—to say farewell to the world and retire to the forest, there to give the remainder of his life to prayer and the thought of God. This was considered to be the duty of all, whatever their station in life, priest and merchant, king and laborer, all alike.
>
> And so in the course of events the great King Bharata, type of the true Hindu sovereign, gave up his wealth and power and withdrew. His family and people woke up one morning, and he was gone. That was all. But everyone understood that . . . he had passed out of the city during the night in the garb of a beggar, and the news spread through the country that his son was king. Just as the water of a lake closes over a stone thrown into it and leaves no trace, so society went on its usual course, and the loss of Bharata made no mark.[13]

---

[12]"Laws of Manu," Chapter VI:2-3, in William H. McNeil and Jean W. Sedlar, *Classical India* (New York: Oxford University Press, 1969), pp. 144-45.
[13]Sister Nivedita, *Cradle Tales of Hinduism* (Calcutta: Advaita Ashrama, 1968), p. 253.

18 ■ THE HINDU TRADITION

Goddess worship is common among Hindus. A goddess is sometimes viewed as the creative energy or force of a god. This colorful image of a goddess is in a temple in Madras.

READING 3
Gods and Goddesses Among the Hindus, Past and Present*

BEATRICE PITNEY LAMB

THE VAST VARIETY OF HINDUISM

The first and most essential point that Westerners must understand is that Hinduism in no way fits into our concept of what a religion is. Most confusingly, it lacks the kinds of signposts which, by our definition, are the very essence of religion. If we ask what a Hindu must believe, the answer is that a very wide diversity of beliefs is not only tolerated, but regarded as natural and normal. According to their different backgrounds or levels of education or personal inclination, Hindus may hold any of a great variety of beliefs. They may believe in an all-pervading God so formless and omnipotent that he cannot be described. Or those who find such a God too difficult to conceive may believe in one or more personal gods with quite human attributes, who are regarded as manifestations of the absolute. For uneducated villagers, there are always the demons, spirits, and godlings of their particular locality who must be propitiated [calmed] through various superstitious practices. But even these main differences do not begin to suggest the wide range and the contrasts within Hinduism. Over the centuries, many highly divergent forms of religious thought have evolved, and these continue to exist

*From Beatrice Pitney Lamb, *India: A World in Transition,* 4th ed. (New York: Praeger Publishers, 1975), pp. 102-9.

vigorously today despite what Westerners might regard as impossible contradictions among them. What then is Hinduism? The only possible answer is that it is a wide variety of beliefs held together by an attitude of mutual tolerance and by the characteristically Hindu conviction that all approaches to God are equally valid. There is no institution or authority, no equivalent of a church or a Pope, to decide matters of belief or to select and determine what religious writings should be included in a commonly accepted canon. Although there is a body of literature generally regarded as sacred, some persons give priority to certain writings, while others give priority to other writings which seem to teach quite different lessons. There is no common scripture corresponding to the Christian Bible or the Muslim Koran.

A man is a Hindu not because of any particular religious belief, but because he was born a Hindu, continues to live within the Hindu social framework, and regards himself as generally committed to a "Hindu way of life." Such a way of life is that laid down not only by one or another of the writings regarded as sacred, but perhaps more especially by the rules and customs of his particular caste or subcaste. If a Hindu departs too far from the Hindu way of life, as viewed by his caste, he may be outcasted—a punishment comparable to excommunication. But this punishment is used to enforce certain standards of behavior rather than of belief.

An important characteristic of Hinduism is that the ideas of "higher" and "lower" are deeply embedded within it. There are "higher" and "lower" beliefs, "higher" and "lower" castes, diets, occupations, marriage customs, and attitudes toward women. Hinduism has tended to grade into a hierarchy everything that it has touched.[1] For example, vegetarianism is regarded by many as "higher" than meat eating, early marriage as "higher" than late marriage, clerical work as "higher" than manual labor. A similar preference for a white-collar job is not, of course, unusual in other cultures; but the distaste for manual labor is particularly strong in India.

Thus, while the Hindu tolerance toward every possible form of belief is so broad that many have called Hinduism "undefined,"

---

[1] M. N. Srinivas, "A Note on Sanskritization and Westernization." *Far Eastern Quarterly,* Vol. XV, No. 4 (August, 1956).

"shapeless," and "amorphous," it has not traditionally been the tolerance of equality. Those who follow the "higher" forms of Hinduism look upon the many "lower" forms of Hinduism as a father might look upon an underdeveloped child. This underlying assumption of inequality has been challenged by the Western doctrine of equality.

Early Hinduism (often called Brahmanism to distinguish it from later Hinduism) stemmed from the religion of the white Aryans who entered India about 1500 B.C. But it gradually incorporated various elements of the religion of the earlier Indus Valley civilization, such as phallic or fertility worship, worship of a mother goddess, and the sanctity of certain trees. The earliest Hindu sacred texts are the Vedas, the hymns and chants of the Aryans, composed in Sanskrit probably about 1500 B.C., but not reduced to writing until perhaps 2,000 years later, long after a script had been invented. Until the Buddhist protest in the sixth century B.C., Hinduism seems to have been the religion of the aristocracy only. It involved elaborate, costly sacrifice and ritual presided over by the Brahmin priestly caste. When Buddhism rose in prominence, Hinduism went into partial eclipse for a number of centuries, although it probably continued to be practiced by many.

The new Hinduism that appeared in the fourth and fifth centuries A.D., after the long interval of Buddhist ascendancy, still placed emphasis on the Vedas but had accepted as legitimate more of the religion of the people than had Brahmanism. In so doing, it had developed its characteristic tolerance of widely different beliefs. It had accepted the cults of invaders subsequent to the Aryans, as well as ancient native cults which apparently had continued to be the religion of the masses despite the Aryan invasions.

But the Brahmins, while finding a place for these cults within their Hindu scheme of things, regarded much of the miscellaneous borrowings as "lower." Even as late as the nineteenth century, both the Vedas and other subsequent sacred writings were the special possession of the Brahmins, who were reluctant to make the study of Sanskrit or the Vedas available to lower castes. Despite this exclusiveness, from the earliest times to the present day there has been a constant exchange and interaction between the "high" Aryan religion and the lower indigenous [native] and non-Aryan cults, many of them local in nature—between what American anthropologists have called the "great tradition" and the "little traditions," more primitive and local in nature. The "higher" religion has been constantly accepting certain ideas, deities, and practices originating in the "lower" cults. Meanwhile, lower castes have tended to take over the religious and cultural ingredients of the "great tradition" whenever they learned what these were. They have imitated not only the ceremonies and ritual of the upper castes, but their social customs as well. This constant tendency toward imitation of the "higher" religion and of the "higher" castes has created a certain degree of unity within the heterogeneous mass of Hinduism. Yet, because there is always a time lag in the process of imitation, it has paradoxically led to increasing attention to "high" Hinduism on the part of many lower- and middle-caste Hindus at the very time that the upper castes, whom they have sought to imitate, have come increasingly under the influence of the West.[2] Thus, in the last century, what might be called Hindu "orthodoxy" has been increasing rather than decreasing as more people have gained access to the Sanskrit texts in the original or in translation.

A child has his hair ritually cut to insure his health and happiness.

VILLAGE CULTS

Only recently have we come to realize that village Hinduism—the Hinduism of close to 85 per cent of the Hindus—is quite different from the Hinduism stemming from the Sanskrit classics. The reason why village Hinduism has remained so largely unknown in the West is that the Hindus whom the British and other Westerners first came to know tended to be of high caste, hence familiar with the religion of the Sanskrit texts rather than the unrecorded practices of the village masses. Today, anthropologists are beginning to tell us what these practices are.

Most Indian villagers know something of the several personal gods who are worshiped by the more educated persons all over India, but their center of attention is still usually focused on a group of local spirits. These spirits—good, evil, or neutral—are not adored or worshiped, but feared. The various rites, cere-

[2]Ibid.

monies, and superstitious practices with which they are approached are attempts to control them and avert their wrath.[3]

The variety of local godlings can only be suggested. In a certain section of south India, a local cult concerns itself with an invisible watchman, Iyenar, who rides on horseback through the countryside at night to ward off evil. Along the roadside, one sees many little clusters of stone or clay horses donated to Iyenar by the villagers as extra mounts to speed him on his way.

Villagers all over India believe in a primitive mother goddess who has different names and requirements in different places. She usually has priests of all castes, requires animal sacrifices, and has crude shrines, often mere heaps of stones rather than temples. She often enters into people as an evil spirit. One of the more common forms of this goddess is that of Mariamma, the Goddess of Smallpox, who either inflicts or wards off this much-dreaded disease. In Mysore, for example, the villagers vigorously deny that smallpox comes through contagion. They believe on the contrary that it comes because the goddess has thrown her pearls about.[4]

None of us, of course, is separated from superstition, magic, witchcraft, and the like by as many generations as we would like to imagine. And even this degree of separation is due not to any inherent superiority but to the good fortune of education and of a safe margin separating us from starvation. Pressed hard by circumstances, Indian villagers must deal in the only way they know with the powerful and dangerous forces by which they feel themselves surrounded.

Sometimes the strongly held superstitions that such cults contain have stood in the way of reforms of agriculture and public health proposed under India's Five-Year Plans. All over India, government agents concerned with the application of science to India's problems have frequently faced the problem of persuading the villagers that the spirit world would not harm them if they abandoned superstitious practices that stood in the way of improved agriculture or better health. Particularly in recent years, however, the villagers have shed their superstitions when they have seen that these conflict with their material well-being.

Villagers gather around a sorceress in northern India.

[3] The Right Reverend Henry Whitehead, *The Village Gods of South India* (London: Oxford University Press, 1921), p. 47.
[4] Unpublished report of Gertrude Woodruff at the Conference of the Association of Asian Studies, March 23, 1959.

THE WORSHIP OF PERSONAL GODS

At a more developed level, Hindu worship centers around various personal gods who are viewed not as rivals but as alternative aspects of the Divine. In the big public temples, where elaborate sculptures remind the worshiper of the many legends connected with the gods, images of the gods are treated as though they were living persons. Priests clothe, feed, and bathe them, and even arrange their marriages. On special occasions, the god, treated as a king, is taken in a parade around the city. These are all symbolic acts. In India, as elsewhere, external ritual has its inner spiritual significance to the worshiper.

But despite these temples and their ceremonies, worship is essentially not congregational. Rather, it is an individual matter to be carried on privately, when and in whatever fashion the worshiper may choose. Every Hindu home has a spot set aside for worship—a puja place with a little ledge for images of the gods and for incense burners, and usually with garlanded pictures of the gods hanging on the wall above.

Religious observance may take place not only at home but also in connection with work. Behind the great drill presses in a diesel-engine factory or on the concrete face of a new dam are little puja places created by the workers themselves. The Indian craftsman conceives of his art not as his own nor as the accumulated skill of the ages, but as originating in the divine skill of his god and revealed by him.[5] In many parts of India, craftsmen still worship their tools during an annual religious festival. The debut of a young professional dancer is essentially a religious ceremony—a consecration of the dancer to her art which itself is religious in its themes and motivation. Passing her palms over flaming camphor, then pressing them together, the young dancer touches her forehead to the ground before her teacher, who gives her the consecrated anklets of bells. (This is the form of the service as performed at the dance school Kalakshetra, in Madras.)

Since the period of Buddhist ascendancy, the two chief personal gods of Hinduism have been Vishnu, the preserver, and Shiva, the creator and destroyer. Vishnu is thought of as having appeared in a number of incarnations and as always being ready to come back to earth when there is a new need for a savior. In one

---

[5]Stella Kramrish, "Traditions of the Indian Craftsman," in Milton Singer (ed.), *Traditional India: Structure and Change* (Philadelphia: American Folklore Society, 1959), p. 18.

of these incarnations, he was born as Krishna, the "divine cowherd" who lived in north India and performed marvelous exploits and miracles recounted in popular legends. His love for the lovely mortal Radha has inspired much music, painting, and poetry. To many Hindus, this love symbolizes the mystical union between the soul and the infinite spirit.

Rama, another of the incarnations of Vishnu, is the subject of one of the two great Hindu epics, the *Ramayana,* which tells of how Rama's wife, Sita, was kidnaped by a demon and carried off to Ceylon. It was only with great difficulty and the help of the monkey Hanuman that Rama finally recovered her. But during the long period when they were separated, she remained faithful to him; she is greatly revered for this as the perfect model of womanhood. Each year in north India, Rama's triumph over the demon Ravana, regarded as symbolic of the eternal triumph of good over evil, is celebrated in a festival lasting ten days and sometimes longer. The entire *Ramayana* is often acted out by local amateur groups. An American anthropologist has noted that in one particular year 321 towns in Uttar Pradesh alone gave such plays.[6] But it is difficult to say just how much of this rich drama of Hinduism should be regarded as religious and how much stems from an enjoyment of entertainment and color which in other societies would take secular forms.

Vishnu, whether worshiped in his own right or in one of his incarnations, is a kindly and consoling god, able to ease the human predicament. The other chief god, Shiva, is more remote, more awesome and terrible. Often depicted dancing surrounded by a circle of flames, he is the god of the eternal, inexorable [unyielding] rhythms of the universe—the dance of life, the ebb and flow, the destruction that makes way for new creation. In his temples, the central image is usually a phallic symbol in stone (lingam). There seems reason to believe that the origins of the worship of Shiva existed in India before the arrival of the Aryans and formed an essential part of the religion of the early Indus Valley civilization.

Not only Krishna and Rama, but also Vishnu and Shiva have wives, and these have many more names than need be noted. A significant number of educated Hindus worship a mother

Ravana, Sita's abductor, will be burned in effigy as the climax to the Rama Lila Festival, celebrated in northern India.

[6]Norvin Hein, "The Ram Lila," in Singer (ed.), op. cit., p. 91.

26 ■ THE HINDU TRADITION

goddess, who seems to be a higher outgrowth of the less developed mother goddess of the Indian countryside—an embodiment of the sustaining primordial [primitive] maternal principle. In certain areas, the goddess, worshiped under the name of Kali, requires blood sacrifices (for example, of goats). Kali is a dread creature, often represented in a horrifying form, with long fangs, wild hair, and a necklace of human skulls. Modern psychologists have made interesting speculations as to what the nature of Kali indicates about the repressed urges of her worshipers.[7]

"HIGH" HINDUISM

For philosphically minded Indians, all personal gods and goddesses are merely aspects or manifestations of the one nameless, indescribable reality that underlies everything. This eternal, universal essence is usually called Brahman (not to be confused with the priestly caste, Brahmin, or with Brahma, one of the personal gods of Hinduism). The supreme Brahman is neuter, impersonal, all-pervading, absolute. The souls of all living things, animal as well as human, are identical with it. It is only ignorance to regard the seeming separateness of objects in the external world as real. The only true reality is oneness in Brahman, and the only right and true purpose in human life is to realize this oneness. Man's essential duty is to transform his consciousness so that he can become one with Brahman.

Of all the contrasting aspects of Hinduism, it is this concept of Brahman that has had the widest influence outside India and has come to seem most characteristic of Hinduism. Within India also, it has had profound influence. Although uneducated Indians may not understand it [the concept of Brahman] and certain schools of Hindu philosophy do not subscribe to it, it forms the basis for many prevalent attitudes and unexamined assumptions.

Like many religious intuitions, the concept of Brahman raises questions that reason finds difficulty in answering. If everything is essentially part of Brahman, what then is matter? What is this hard earth on which we stand, this tree that we touch, this ego which urgently wants its own desires fulfilled? Some Hindu thinkers have answered that such things exist only in a relative sense, as

Vishnu (upper left) is worshipped as the protector of the world. Ganesha (upper right) is considered the remover of obstacles and is frequently found at temple and house entrances. The goddess Durga (lower left) is shown here killing the buffalo demon. Shiva (lower right), the supreme deity of the Shaiva sect, is shown here as the lord of the dance.

[7] See, for example, G. Morris Carstairs, *The Twice Born* (London: Hogarth Press, 1957), p. 158.

emanations of Brahman; since Brahman alone exists, all that is merely relative is known as maya (illusion). Others tend to grant at least a partial reality to matter and to individual selves, arguing that Brahman can be present in such objects in various degrees.

Hence, between pure matter at one end of the cosmic scale and pure spirit at the other, there is a gradual ascent—from the inorganic to the organic, from mere life to consciousness, from consciousness to reason, and from reason to spiritual perfection and the Supreme Spirit. The great purpose in life should be to enhance spiritual values, to free the spirit from the drag of matter, to realize the spirit within one's self.

In order to do this, man should choose the god best suited to his understanding and subject himself to rigorous discipline.

READING 4
How Many Gods?*

Then Vidagdha Sakalya asked him: 'How many gods are there, O Yagnavalkya?' He replied with this very Nivid [formula]: 'As many as are mentioned in the Nivid of the hymn of praise addressed to the Visvedevas, viz. three and three hundred, three and three thousand.'

'Yes,' he said, and asked again: 'How many gods are there really, O Yagnavalkya?'

'Thirty-three,' he said.

'Yes,' he said, and asked again: 'How many gods are there really, O Yagnavalkya?'

'Six,' he said.

'Yes,' he said, and asked again: 'How many gods are there really, O Yagnavalkya?'

'Three,' he said.

'Yes,' he said, and asked again: 'How many gods are there really, O Yagnavalkya?'

'Two,' he said.

'Yes,' he said, and asked again: 'How many gods are there really, O Yagnavalkya?'

'One and a half (adhyardha),' he said.

'Yes,' he said, and asked again: 'How many gods are there really, O Yagnavalkya?'

'One,' he said.

'Yes,' he said, and asked: 'Who are these three and three hundred, three and three thousand?'

Yagnavalkya, replied: 'They are only the various powers. . . .'

*From *The Upanishads,* Part II, trans. by F. Max Muller in *The Sacred Books of the East,* vol. XV (Oxford: Clarendon Press, 1884).

A Nepalese Hindu holy man. The trident in his hand and paint on his forehead identify him as a follower of Shiva.

READING 5
The Goals of Hindu Life*
HUSTON SMITH

THE WANTS OF MAN

If we were to take Hinduism as a whole—its vast literature, its lavish art, its elaborate rituals, its sprawling folkways—if we were to take this enormous outlook in its entirety and sum it up in a single, central affirmation we would find it saying to man: You can have what you want.

This sounds good but it throws the problem back in our laps. For what *do* we want? It is easy to give a simple answer but hard to give a good one. India has been with this question a long time, and has her answer waiting. The wants of man, she says, are four.

He begins by wanting pleasure. This is natural. We are all born with built-in pleasure-pain reactors. If we ignored these completely, leaving our hands on hot stoves or stepping out of second-story windows, we would read ourselves out of existence. What could be more obvious, then, than to follow these friendly leads of pleasure and make them our guiding principle and ultimate goal?

Having heard—for this is a common Western view—that India is ascetic, other-worldly, and life-denying, we might expect her attitude toward hedonists, who set pleasure as their goal, to be sharply scolding, but it is not. True, India has not taken pleasure as life's highest value, but this is different from condemning enjoyment as itself evil. To the person who wants pleasure, India

---

*Adapted from Huston Smith, *The Religions of Man* (New York: Harper & Row, 1958), pp. 16–29.

says in effect: Go after it—there is nothing wrong with it. It is one of the four legitimate ends of life. The world holds immense possibilities for enjoyment. It is flooded with beauty and heavy with delights for all our senses. Moreover, there are other worlds above this where pleasures mount by a factor of a million at each successive round; we shall experience these worlds too at later stages in our becoming. Of course, hedonism like everything else calls for good sense. Not every impulse can be followed without possible harm; small immediate goals must be sacrificed for the sake of greater future ones, and impulses that would injure others must be checked if for no other reason than to avoid antagonisms without and a troubled conscience within. Only the ignorant will lie, steal, or cheat for the sake of seeming advantage or fall into gross addictions. But as long as the basic rules of morality are observed you are free to seek all the pleasure you wish. Far from condemning pleasure, Hindu texts abound in pointers on how to increase it to the full. For the simple peasant whose aspirations are still in this direction, virtually all religion, from its rites and rituals to its ethical dictates, is presented as something that can protect his prosperity and good fortune, bring rain, heal the sick, and in general insure good fortune. Even for the sophisticate, there is in accepted Hindu philosophy a hedonism which, in its combined subtlety and frankness, often shocks the West. If pleasure is what you want, says India, don't suppress this desire. See instead that it is fulfilled as richly and esthetically as possible.

She says this—and waits. She waits for the time (it will come to everyone, though not to everyone in his present life) when one realizes that pleasure *isn't* all one wants. The reason everyone eventually comes to this discovery is not because pleasure is wicked—we have seen that it is not—but because it is weakening and too narrow and trivial to satisfy man's total nature. Pleasure is essentially private, and the self is too small an object for perpetual enthusiasm. . . . Sooner or later, everyone wants to be more than a kaleidoscope of private, momentary pleasures however exquisite and subtle.

When this time comes the individual's interests usually shift to the second great goal of life which is worldly success,[1] with its

---

[1] The Sanskrit word here is *artha* which literally means "thing, object, substance" and so is usually translated "wealth" or "material possessions." I have translated it "worldly success" because the Hindu texts when discussing this second pursuit deal in fact with this larger theme, not just wealth, which is natural considering the usual connection of prestige and power with material possessions.

three aspects of wealth, fame, and power. This too is a worthy goal, to be neither scorned nor condemned. Moreover its satisfactions last longer, for, unlike pleasure, success is a social achievement substantially meshed with the lives of others. . . .

This point does not have to be argued for an American audience. The Anglo-American world is not voluptuous; visitors from other cultures are almost unanimous in their impression that, despite superficial appearances to the contrary, English-speaking peoples do not enjoy life a great deal and are not really intent upon doing so—they are in too much of a hurry. The impress of Calvinism and Puritanism is still deep. What has conquered the West is the gospel not of sensualism but of success. What takes arguing for the West is not that achievement carries rewards beyond sensualism but rather that success too has its limitations, that man has never been able to live by bread alone and that the question "What is he worth?" can have a deeper reference than "How much has he got?"

India acknowledges that drives for possessions, status, and power run deep. Nor should they be minimized per se. A bit of worldly success is indispensable for the upkeep of a household, raising a family, and discharge of civic duties. Beyond this minimum, worldly achievements bring to many a sense of dignity and self-respect. In the end, however, these too are found wanting. For beneath the surface of each lurk the following limitations:

1. Wealth, fame, and power are exclusive, hence competitive, hence risky. Unlike values associated more directly with man's mind and spirit, these do not multiply when shared; they cannot be distributed without one's own portion being diminished. If I own a dollar, that dollar cannot be yours. As long as I am sitting on a chair, you cannot sit on it too. Fame and power are similarly exclusive. The idea of a nation in which everyone is famous is a contradiction in terms; if power were distributed equally no one would be powerful in the sense in which we customarily use the word. Fame consists in standing out from one's fellows and power is control over them. From the competitiveness of these values to their riskiness is a short step. As other people of ability want them too, who knows when success will change hands? One can never be certain that one's competitors will not gain the advantage; hence a position of unquestionable security is never reached.

2. The second contradiction within worldly success when this is taken as life's objective is the sense in which it can never be satisfied. While it is not true to say that men can never get enough money, fame, and power, it is true to say that men can never get enough of these things when they want them greedily, when they make them the supreme forces of their lives. These are not the things men really want, and man can never get enough of what he does not really want. As the Hindus say, "to try to extinguish the drive for riches with money is like trying to quench a fire by pouring butterfat over it."

The West, too, has of course known this point well. "Poverty consists, not in the decrease of one's possessions, but in the increase of one's greed," writes Plato for the philosophers. "Could you from all the world all wealth procure, more would remain, whose lack would leave you poor," adds St. Gregory Nazianzen for the theologians. Abram Kardiner speaks for the psychologists, "Success is a goal without a satiation point," while the Lynds in their first sociological study of Middletown note that "both business men and working men seem to be running for dear life in this business of making the money they earn keep pace with the even more rapid growth of their subjective wants." Each of these men is testifying from his own professional perspective to the point India, characteristically, puts in a parable, the parable of the donkey before which the driver dangled a luscious carrot hanging from a stick fastened to its own harness. The more the animal ran to get the carrot, the further the carrot receded.

3. The third weakness of worldly success is identical with that of hedonism. Though less obviously trivial than pleasure, it too centers value and meaning in the self which must eventually be sensed in the silences of subjectivity to be too small for the heart's eternal trust. Neither fortune nor position can shut out the awareness that the possessor lacks so much else....

4. The final reason worldly success cannot satisfy man completely is because its achievements are short-lived. Man knows well that wealth, fame, and power do not survive bodily death. "You can't take it with you," has become the familiar way of putting this point in the West. And since he cannot, this fact must keep these things from satisfying man wholly, for he is a creature who can envision eternity and must instinctively regret by contrast the brief purchase on time his worldly successes command.

Before proceeding to the other two things Hinduism sees men wanting it will be well to summarize the ones considered thus far. Pleasure and success are described by the Hindus as the twin goals of the Path of Desire. They use this phrase because the personal desires of the individual have thus far been uppermost in charting life's course. Other goals lie ahead but this does not mean that our attitude toward the ones already recounted should be negative. Nothing can possibly be gained by repressing desires wholesale or pretending we do not have them. As long as pleasure and success are what we think we want we should go after them, remembering only the means of caution and fair play already noted.

A sadhu, or religious ascetic, reads by the Ganges River. A sadhu *is a person who has left the comforts of home in order to cultivate physical and spiritual disciplines.*

In short, Hinduism regards the objects of the Path of Desire as if they were toys. If we ask ourselves whether there is anything wrong with toys our answer must be: on the contrary, there is something tragic in the picture of children deprived of them. Even sadder, however, is that of adults who fail to move on to interests more significant than dolls and electric trains. A mature adult takes interest in such things not from his own need but for the sake of children who prize them and move through their enjoyment of them to a point beyond. By the same token, in the perspective of man's total career the individual whose development is not arrested will work his way through full delight in success and the senses to the point where these pulls have been largely outgrown. Unless he does, his energies must remain locked forever in life's trite, outmoded nursery.

But what more significant concerns does life afford? Two, answers Hinduism. In contrast with the Path of Desire, they make up the Path of Renunciation.

The word renunciation has a negative ring, and India's frequent use of it has undoubtedly been one of the factors in earning for her the reputation of being life-denying and pessimistic. Renunciation, however, can be prompted by disillusionment and despair, in which case it represents life's foreclosing, the liquidation proceedings of the human spirit in withdrawal and decline. But renunciation can also be a clearer sign of exhilaration and confidence in life's high calling than any amount of momentary indulgence. In this category falls discipline of every form, the sacrifice of a trivial now for a momentous then, the turning away from an easy this toward a beckoning yet-to-be. When not perverted, religious renunciation is on a continuum with that of the athlete in training who turns his back upon every indulgence that would deflect from his prize. Precisely the opposite of disillusionment, it is the only evidence that can be given of life's confidence in the existence of values beyond those it is experiencing at the moment.

We must never forget that in Hinduism the Path of Renunciation comes *after* the Path of Desire. If men could be satisfied by following their initial wants the idea of renunciation would never have arisen. Nor does it occur only to those who have failed on the former path—the young man who enters a monastery because he has been jilted, for example. We can agree with those who belittle renunciation that such persons may resort to it only to rationalize or to compensate for personal inadequacies. What forces us to listen attentively to Hinduism's hypothesis of other goals is the testimony of those who have followed the Path of Desire with brilliant success only to find themselves wishing desperately that life could give them something more. These people—not the ones who renounce but the ones who see nothing to renounce for—are the world's real pessimists. For to live a man must believe in that for the sake of which he lives. If he sees no futility in pleasure and success he can believe in these as worth living for. But if, as Tolstoy points out in his *Confession,* he can no longer have faith in the value of the finite, he will believe in the infinite or die.

. . .Hinduism does not say that everyone in his present life will find the Path of Desire inadequate. For against a vaster time scale Hinduism draws a distinction with which we have all become familiar between chronological and psychological age. Two men both forty-six are the same age chronologically but psychologically one may be still a child whereas the other is a mature adult. The Hindus accept this distinction but extend it to cover multiple life spans. . . .We will, consequently, find men and women who play the game of desire with all the zest of nine-year-olds at cops and robbers; though they know nothing else they will die with the sense of having lived to the full and will leave as their verdict that life is good. But equally there will be others who play this game just as ably yet find the laurels inadequate. Why the difference? The difference, say the Hindus, lies in the fact that the enthusiasts are caught in the flush of novelty whereas the others, having played and won the game more often, are instinctively feeling out for other worlds to conquer.

We can describe the typical experience of this second type. The world's visible rewards still attract him strongly. He throws himself into enjoyment, building up his holdings and advancing his status. But neither the pursuit nor the attainment of these things brings him true happiness. Some of the things he wants he fails to get and this makes him miserable. Some he gets and holds for a while only to have them suddenly snatched from him—and again he is miserable. Some he both gets and keeps only to find, like the experience of so many Christmases in adolescence, that they do not bring the joy he expected. Many experiences that thrilled on first encounter lose their attraction on the hundredth.

Throughout, each attainment seems only to fan the fire of new desire; none satisfies fully and all, he perceives, perish with time. Eventually there comes over him a suspicion that he is caught on a nonstop treadmill, having to race faster and faster for rewards that mean less and less.

When this condition is reached and he finds himself crying, "Vanity, vanity, all is vanity!" it may occur to him that his trouble lies in the fact that his satisfactions are limited by the smallness of the self he has been scrambling to serve. What if the focus of his concern were shifted? Might not becoming a part of a larger, more significant whole relieve his life of its oppressive triviality?

This question, once it arises, brings the beginning of religion. For though in some watered-down sense there may be a religion which makes of the self its own god, true religion begins with the quest for meaning and value beyond privacy—with renunciation of the ego's claims to finality.

But for what is this renunciation to be made? The question brings us to the two specific ingredients in the Path of Renunciation. The human community suggests itself as the first candidate. In supporting at once our own life and the lives of myriads of others, the community has an importance no single life can command. Let us, then, transfer our allegiance to it, giving its claims priority over our own.

This is the first step in religion. It produces the religion of duty, the third great aim of life in the Hindu outlook. Its power over those who have matured enough to feel its pull is tremendous. Countless persons have passed beyond the wish to win into the wish to be of service, beyond the wish to gain to the wish to give. Not to triumph but to do their best, to acquit themselves as men in whatever task life puts before them, has become their deepest objective.

Hinduism abounds in directives to the man or woman who would put his shoulder to the human enterprise. It sets forth in elaborate detail the duties which go with age, disposition, and social status. . . . We need only repeat for this third life-objective what was said in connection with the previous two: it, too, yields notable rewards, but in the end fails to satisfy the human heart completely. Its rewards require maturity to be appreciated, but given this they are substantial. Faithful performance of duty brings the praise of peers. More gratifying than this, however, is

A memorial to Mahatma Gandhi, who is considered the father of modern India. Gandhi advocated nonviolence to achieve political and social progress. The title Mahatma *means "Great Soul."*

the self-respect that comes from having done one's part, of having contributed. But in the end even this realization cannot provide joy adequate to man's desiring. For even when extended through history, the human community, as long as it stands alone, remains both finite and tragic; tragic not only in the sense that it must eventually come to an end, but also in its inflexible resistance to perfection. The final want of man must still lie elsewhere.

WHAT MEN REALLY WANT

"There comes a time," writes Aldous Huxley, "when one asks even of Shakespeare, even of Beethoven, is this all?"

It is difficult to think of a sentence that puts its finger more precisely on Hinduism's attitude toward the world. The things of this world are not bad. By and large they are good. Some of them are so wonderful that they can command man's admiration and enthusiasm for many life-times. Eventually, however, every human being comes to realize with Simone Weil "that there is no true good here below, that everything that appears to be good in this world is finite, limited, wears out, and once worn out, leaves necessity exposed in all its nakedness."[2] When this point is reached, he will find himself asking even of the finest this world can offer—not only the peaks of esthetic experience but the highest reaches of love and knowledge and duty as well— "Is this all?"

This is the moment Hinduism has been waiting for. As long as a person is content with the prospects of pleasure, success, or dutiful living, the Hindu sage will not be likely to disturb him beyond offering some suggestions as to how to proceed toward these goals more effectively. The critical point in life comes when these things lose their original charm and one finds oneself wishing that life had something more to offer. Whether life does or does not hold more is probably the question which divides men more sharply than any other.

The [Hindu] answer to this question is clear. Life definitely holds other possibilities. To see what these are we must return to the question of what men want. Thus far, Hinduism would say, we

[2] *Waiting for God* (New York: G. P. Putnam's Sons, 1951), p. 210.

have been answering this question too superficially. Pleasure, success, and duty are never man's ultimate goals; at best they are means which we assume will take us in the direction of what we really want. What we really want are things which lie on a deeper level.

First, we want being. Everyone wants to be rather than not be. Normally nobody wants to die. Toward the close of his own life, Ernie Pyle, the great correspondent of World War II, described the atmosphere of a room in which were gathered thirty-five men who had been assigned to a bombing mission the following day. On an average only one-fourth of those who went out on this particular run returned. What he felt in those men, Ernie Pyle wrote, was not really fear. Rather, it was "a profound reluctance to give up the future." This is true of us all, the Hindus would say; none of us takes happily to the thought of the future proceeding without us. Occasionally an individual may find himself driven by desperation to suicide but no one really feels happy about dying.

Second, we want to know, to be aware. People are endlessly curious. Whether it be a scientist probing the mysteries of nature, a businessman scanning the morning paper, a teen-ager glued to television to find out who won the ball game, or neighbors catching up on the local news over a cup of coffee, our curiosity is never satisfied. Experiments have shown that monkeys will work longer and harder to find out what is on the other side of a trap door than they will for rewards of either food or sex. If curiosity is this strong in monkeys, how much stronger in human beings!

The third thing men seek is joy, a resolution of feelings in which the basic themes are the opposite of frustration, futility, and boredom.

These are the real desires of men. To which if we are to complete the picture, says Hinduism, we must add one further point. Not only are these the things man wants; he wants each of them in infinite degree. One of the most distinctive and significant features of man is the fact that he can conceive the idea of infinity. This capacity colors his entire life, as di Chirico's painting "Nostalgia of the Infinite" poignantly suggests. Mention any good and man can always imagine a bit more of it and in doing so wish for that more. Medical science has doubled man's life expectancy, but is man today more ready to die once that expectancy is reached? To state the full truth, then, we must say that what man

Women in courtyard of a Hindu temple at Udaipur, India.

would really like is infinite being, infinite knowledge, and infinite joy. Disregarding for the moment what he might have to settle for, these are what he would really like. To gather them together in a single word, what man really wants is liberation (*mukti*)—complete release from the countless limitations that press so closely upon his present existence.

Pleasure, success, responsible discharge of duty, and liberation—we have completed the circuit of what man thinks he wants and what he really wants. And now we come back to India's staggering conclusion with which we began; what man most wants, that he can have. Infinite being, infinite awareness, and infinite joy are within his reach. The most startling statement, however, comes next. Not only are these within his reach, Hinduism argues; they are already his.

For what is man? A body? Certainly, but anything else? A personality that includes his mind, memories, and the tendencies that have accumulated from his own unique pattern of life experiences? This, too, but anything more? Some would say no, but Hinduism disagrees. Underlying man's personality and animating it is a reservoir of being that never dies, is never exhausted, and is without limit in awareness and bliss. This infinite center of every life, this hidden self or *Atman,* is no less than *Brahman,* the God-head. Body, personality, and *Atman-Brahman*—man is not completely accounted for until all three have been named.

But if this is true, if we really are infinite in our being, why is this not apparent? Why do we not act accordingly? "I don't happen to feel particularly unlimited today," one may be prompted to observe. "And my neighbor—I haven't noticed his behavior as exactly Godlike." How can the Hindu thesis possibly withstand the evidence of the morning paper?

The answer, say the Hindus, lies in the extent to which the Eternal is buried under the almost impenetrable mass of distractions, false ideas, and self-regarding impulses that comprise our surface being. A lamp may be so covered with dust and dirt that its light will be invisible. The problem life puts to man is to cleanse the impurity of his being to the point where its infinite center will be fully manifest.

This, clearly, is a thesis that must be explored further.

THE BEYOND THAT IS WITHIN

"The aim of life," Justice Holmes used to say, "is to get as far as possible from imperfection." Hinduism says its purpose is to pass beyond imperfection altogether.

If we were to set out to compile a catalogue of the specific imperfections that limit our lives, it would have no end. We lack strength and imagination to effect our dreams; we fall ill; we grow tired; we make mistakes; we are ignorant; we fall and become discouraged; we grow old and die. Lists of this sort could be extended indefinitely but there is no need, for all specific limitations reduce to three basic variants. We are limited in being, knowledge, and joy, the three things men really want.

Is it possible to pass beyond the limitations that separate us from these things? Is it feasible to seek to rise to a quality of life which, because less defined, would be life indeed?

The limitations on our joy fall into three groups: physical pain, the frustration from the thwarting of desire, and boredom with life as a whole. The first is the least troublesome. As its intensity is due in large part to the fear which accompanies it, the conquest of fear can reduce pain appreciably. When seen to have a purpose, pain can be accepted, as one welcomes the return of life and feeling to a frozen arm even though painful. Again, pain can be forgotten in the urgency of purpose. In extreme cases of useless pain it may be possible simply to turn it off through anesthesia induced either externally through drugs or internally through mastery of the senses. Ramakrishna, the greatest Hindu saint of the nineteenth century, died of cancer of the throat. A doctor who was examining him in the last stages of this dreadful disease probed the degenerating tissue and Ramakrishna started in pain. "Wait a minute," he said, then, "Go ahead." After which the doctor could probe without resistance. He had placed himself in a state of mind in which the nerve sensations did not break through on his awareness at all or barely did so. One way or another it seems possible to rise to a point where physical pain ceases to be a serious limitation.

Far more serious is the psychological pain which arises from the thwarting of specific desires. We want to win a golf tournament but don't; we want to make money on a deal but lose; we want to be promoted but are not; we want to be invited but are snubbed. Life is so filled with disappointments that we are likely to assume that they are embedded in the condition of being human. As we look, however, we discover something all disappointments share in common. Each lets down some personal expectation of the individual ego. If the ego were to have no expectations, there would then be nothing to disappoint.

Or, if this sounds like ending an ailment by killing the patient, put the same point in positive terms. What if the interests of the self were expanded to the point of approximating a God's-eye view of the human scene. Seeing, thus, all things "under the aspect of eternity," would not one become completely objective toward oneself, accepting failure as being as natural an occurrence as success in the stupendous human drama of yes and no, positive and negative, push and pull—as little cause for worry and concern as having to play the role of a loser in a summer theater performance? How can defeat disappoint if one feels the joy of the victor as if it were one's own? How can failure to be promoted touch one if the rival's success can be enjoyed vicariously with equal force? Instead of crying "Impossible" we ought perhaps to content ourselves with observing how different this would be from life as it is usually lived, for the lives of the greatest spiritual geniuses suggest that they rose to precisely this condition. "Inasmuch as ye have done it unto the least of these, ye have done it unto me." Are we to suppose that Jesus was posturing when he uttered these words? We are told that Ramakrishna once

> howled with pain when he saw two boatmen quarrelling angrily. He came to identify himself with the sorrows of the whole world, however impure and murderous they might be, until his heart was scored with scars. But he knew that even the differences leading to strife among men are the daughters of the same Mother; that the 'Omnipotent Differentiation' is the face of God Himself; that he must love God in all sorts and conditions of men, however antagonistic and hostile, and in all forms of thought controlling their existence and often setting them at variance one with the other.[3]

Detachment from the finite self or attachment to reality as a whole—we can state the phenomenon in either positive or negative terms. When it occurs life is lifted above the possibility of frustration. Above a feeling of dissatisfaction as well, for the

---

[3] D. G. Mukerji, *The Face of Silence* as paraphrased in Romain Rolland, *The Life of Ramakrishna* (Mayavati, Almora, Himalayas: Advaita Ashrama, 1954), p. 80.

cosmic drama is too spectacular to permit boredom in the face of such intensive identification.

The second great limitation of human life is ignorance. The Hindus claim this, too, is removable. The *Upanishads* speak of "knowing That the knowledge of which brings knowledge of everything." It is difficult to know whether this means that there is a discovery which, if made, would bring literally a detailed simultaneous awareness of everything that has ever happened or ever will. More likely it refers to some blinding insight which so illumines the cosmic scene that its stupendous point is laid bare. In the presence of this shattering vision of wholeness, to ask of details would be as irrelevant as asking the number of atoms in a particular patch of blue in a Picasso painting, or the number of vibrations per second in the lowest note of a chord climaxing a Bach chorale. When the point is grasped, who cares about details?

But is transcendent knowledge even in this second sense open to man? Certainly the mystics are unanimous in their reports that it is. Academic psychology has not followed their claims all the way and often seems to look in a different direction, but it too has become convinced that there is far more to our minds than we see on the surface. Our minds are like icebergs, most of which lie below the waterline of visibility. What lies in this vast, submerged continent we call the subconscious? Some think it harbors every memory and experience that has come to us, absolutely nothing being lost to this deep mind that never sleeps. Others like Carl Jung think it includes racial memories, a collective unconscious that summarizes the wisdom of the human race. The purpose of psychoanalysis is to throw a few pinpoints of light onto those vast, opaque regions of our minds that are invisible until specially approached. But suppose this submerged continent could be fully conquered. Who can predict how far the horizons of our awareness would be pushed back?

As for life's third limitation, that of being, to profitably consider this we have first to ask how the boundary of the self is to be defined. Not, certainly, by the amount of physical space our bodies occupy, the amount of water we displace when we submerge in the bathtub. It would make more sense if we were to gauge a man's being by the size of his spirit, that is, the range of reality with which he identifies himself. A man who identifies himself with his family, finding his joys in theirs, would have that much reality; one who could really identify himself with mankind as a whole would be proportionately greater. By this criterion, if a man could identify himself with being in general, being as a whole, his own being would be unlimited. Still this seems hardly right, for no extent of such identification could keep him from dying at which time his being would be cut off abruptly. The object of his concern would continue, but he would be gone.

We need, therefore, to approach this question of being not only spatially, so to speak, but also in terms of time. Our everyday experience provides a wedge for doing so. Strictly speaking every moment in our lives is a dying. The I of that moment dies, never to live again. Yet despite the fact that in this sense my experience consists of nothing but funerals, I do not think that I am dying in these, for I do not equate myself with any one of my experiences. I think of myself enduring through these, witnessing them, but not in my entirety identical with any. Hinduism pushes this concept back to another level. It affirms a self that underlies my entire present life as that endures through my individual experiences.

A child's heart is broken by misfortunes we consider trivial. He *is* each incident, being unable to see it against the backdrop of a whole, variable lifetime. A great deal of experience is required before the child shifts his self-identification away from the individual moment and becomes an adult. Compared with children we are mature, but compared with saints we are children. No more capable of seeing our total selves in perspective than a three-year-old who has broken her doll, our attention is fixated on our present lifespan. If only we could grow up completely we would discover that our total being is more vast than we suppose. We would find that it is infinite.

This is the basic point in the Hindu estimate of man. Contemporary psychology, as we have seen, has accustomed us to the fact that there is more to ourselves than we suspect. Like the earth of a hundred years ago, our minds have . . . their unmapped Borneos and Amazonian basins. Indeed, their bulk still waits for exploration. According to Hinduism, mind's hidden continents spread until they touch infinity. Infinite in being, infinite in awareness, there is nothing outside them waiting to be known. Infinite in joy, too, for again there is nothing external or contradictory which could intrude to interrupt their eternal self-content.

Hindu literature is full of parables and metaphors designed to open our imaginations to this infinite which lies concealed in the depths of every life. We are like a king who, falling victim to amnesia, wanders his kingdom in tatters not knowing who he really is. We are like a lion cub who, having become lost from his mother at birth, grows up by accident among sheep and takes to grazing and bleating like them, assuming that he too is a sheep. We are like a lover who, dreaming, searches the world in despair for his beloved, oblivious to the fact that she is lying at his side.

What the realization of our total being is like can be known only by actual experience; it can no more be described than a sunset to one born blind. The biographies of those who have made this supreme discovery provide us, however, with important clues. These men are wiser; they have more personal strength and joy. They seem free, not in the sense that they go around breaking the laws of nature (though the power to do exceptional things which could only seem like miracles to us is usually ascribed to them) but in the sense that they never find the natural order frustrating. This being so, nothing binds them nor shakes them. Nothing disrupts their peace of mind. They feel no lack, no misery, no fear, and find no cause for strife or grief. They seem always to be in good spirits, agreeable, even gay. As their egos need no bolstering, their love can flow outward, alike to all. Contact with them imparts strength, purity, and encouragement.

READING 6
Caste*
HERBERT STROUP

A very special feature of Indian life, enforced by Hinduism, is caste. Actually the word is not Indian; it is derived from the Portuguese word, *casta,* for race, breed, or kind. No one word for caste exists in the native languages in India, although the existence of caste is almost everywhere recognized and followed. So extensive is caste that it not only embraces Hindus but also influences some Muslim, Christian, and other groups as well. Despite its importance in Indian society, no one knows for sure how it originated. Mythologically it is said not to have existed at the beginning of human time. Then everyone belonged to the same class. This was at the time of the *krita-yuga,* or first age. The whole class or caste was called the *hamsa.* But in the following ages mankind deteriorated and immorality increased, so that in various successive ages the several castes came into existence. The brahmins, it is said, still retain some of the traces of their being derived from the *hamsa.*

Another version of the origins of caste points to the Rig Veda hymn, the Purusha-sukta, the nineteenth hymn and the twelfth verse in Mandala X, which is thought by some scholars to be a late addition. This verse says that the castes were divinely created. Here the fourfold division of society is related to the physical features of Purusha. The brahmin was the god's mouth, the

*Adapted from Herbert Stroup, *Like a Great River: An Introduction to Hinduism* (New York: Harper & Row, 1972), pp. 151–58.

kshatriya was his arms, the *vaishya* was his thighs, and the *shudra* was his feet. This verse is remarkable for many reasons, but among them is the fact that it is very often quoted, especially by high-caste Hindus, and also by reason of the further fact that the verse's sentiment has been taken with gross variations as a divinely prescribed sanction of a social system for a nation of great population which is without parallel in human history. In addition to this verse, however, there exist in Hinduism a number of important documents which also reinforce the importance of the caste arrangements. . . .Probably the idea of the fourfold division of society as a model was largely the creation of the composer of the Laws of Manu, although obviously the writer of the laws also was influenced by accounts of caste already existing in his time and previously.

Many theories exist that seek to explain the origins of caste in India on a nonreligious basis, but these are in nature more suggestive than conclusive. One theory suggests that conquest and *varna,* or color of skin, account for caste. It is asserted that the Aryan invaders were dominantly lighter skinned than the local peoples and that the caste system reflects the divinely based social rationale by which the conquerors assigned persons in the new society. The Aryans became the top three castes, while the conquered became the fourth, or *shudra,* caste. But there are drawbacks to this theory. A brahmin, for example, may generally be of lighter skin, yet even a jet-black brahmin is a brahmin. His caste is not determined solely by his color. Again, the Aryans seem not to have dominated the east and south of India, yet in those places the caste system is quite strong, suggesting perhaps that it did not have an exclusively Aryan base.

Another theory proposes that caste derived from certain occupational distinctions that arose early in Indian history. According to the Laws of Manu, each caste has specialized responsibilities: the brahmin studies, teaches, sacrifices, gives and receives gifts; the *kshatriya* protects the people, sacrifices, and studies; the *vaishya* studies and sacrifices, but he also tills the soil, breeds cattle, trades, and lends money; and the *shudra* has only the duty of serving the three higher castes. The subdivisions within each caste, moreover, tend to reinforce this theory, for to a very large extent they are based on occupational distinctions. Yet this theory too has its deficiencies. Agriculture, for example, is an

These Brahmins are participating in a mass bathing ceremony.

occupation that is widely practiced by members of several castes. A number of castes have priests who are not brahmins. The more narrow definition of the duties of the *kshatriya,* or warrior caste, has largely disappeared. Many government workers are not members of this caste, nor are many members of the armed forces. This theory, then, like many others is partially helpful in explaining the origins of caste, but it cannot be pressed too hard. Probably a combination of factors best accounts for the rise of caste. . . .

The fourfold caste division of Indian society has historically been mainly an ideal. There have been times when it has been realized to greater and less degrees. . . .But the fourfold division in reality is replaced by a much more complex system in which a large number of castes and subcastes are found. No one knows with surety the exact number of castes and subcastes at the present time. Some authorities say that there are as many as three thousand castes and more than 25,000 subcastes. . . .

No matter how it originated, caste in India's long history and even today is a fact. It is probably the most significant influence upon individual and collective behavior. While its influence is great, it is difficult to encompass within exception-proof categories. Yet some of its basic characteristics may be outlined with a certain assurance that they are common features of the social system. First, the caste system is endogamous [that is, members of a caste do not marry outside their caste]. Perhaps most basically it provides for groups of families in which the members can marry each other. This means that the system is hereditary in that a person's place in society is determined not by his own efforts but, rather, by the place of his parents. In general it means that one cannot marry up, that is, use marriage as a device for social climbing. Thus the caste system has maintained a kind and degree of social stability for India which is remarkable. Second, caste is marked by commensality [eating restrictions]. This restriction signifies that food may be received from and eaten in the presence of members of the same caste or a higher caste. Sometimes this limit is spoken of as a prohibition against interdining. Members of different castes are regulated not only in the social experience of eating, but in other social relationships. It restricts the distances which various castes are required to maintain from other castes. For example, a member of one subcaste may be required to remain thirty-six paces from a brahmin and only twelve from a member of another subcaste. Where distances are difficult to keep, such as in a teeming metropolitan area, the restriction against members of different castes physically touching each other may still be retained.

Third, caste to a large extent holds to work exclusiveness. Each caste and subcaste is characterized by a particular vocational basis. Each caste member assumes the work of his caste. Over many years the caste specialization of work has led to a fairly traditional form of economy in which the interests and the skills of the father are passed to the son without regard to the overall social needs. But it also has led to highly developed skills within accepted occupations, for the generations have been able to teach the young in the family regarding techniques of production that otherwise might be lost.

Fourth, caste is characterized by graded relationships among the several castes. The castes and their subcastes are not equally regarded; each holds a position of social regard in relation to the others. So the members of a subcaste will in general be well aware of the position of their subcaste in relation to the other subcastes around them. They will know whether their subcaste is inferior, superior, or equal to another subcaste. The *sonar* (goldsmith), in this arrangement, is superior to the *sutar* (carpenter). The *sutar*, on the other hand, is superior to the *goala* (milkman) even as the latter is superior to the *teli* (oil merchant).

In addition to these four basic characteristics of caste, other points of distinction also hold to a greater or less degree. Traditionally, for example, the three highest castes are said to be twice-born. They are born first at birth, but they are born a second time when they complete a ceremony in youth in which they are invested with their special standing. As twice-born persons they are entitled to study the Vedas, perform sacrifices, and enter into the *asramas,* or formal stages of life-development. The *shudra,* or lowest caste member, is only once-born and he is not permitted the privileges of the others. Theoretically the castes are also differentiated on the basis of certain external expressions. Each caste has its own distinctive color: white for the *brahmim,* red for the *kshatriya,* yellow for the *vaishya,* and black for the *shudra.* Caste members use these colors for their dress or for some ornamentation of their dress and for their homes. A number of religious elements also distinguish the castes. While the *shudra* has virtually none, the other castes have special times for family ceremonies, ages when they begin their religious studies, special festivals, and so forth. In the twice-born ceremony, for example, the brahmin is invested with a thread of a special grass, the *kshatriya* with a bow-string, and the *vaishya* with wool or hemp. Sometimes in the villages the well from which the villagers gather water may be the focus of distinction. Caste members may all be able to draw water from a well, while nonmembers or outcastes may be prohibited. In some cases, where only one well is available, members of the castes may draw from one side of the well and nonmembers from the other side. One's relationship, then, to the use of a well may reflect one's caste membership.

Each caste or subcaste has a high degree of self-awareness and enforces its own requirements through a caste council. Questions that may arise regarding caste membership, especially through the presentation of new or exceptional circumstances, are settled by the council. The individual member of a caste or subcaste is guided by his own conscience and by well-known and well-enforced standards for behavior. The dangers of contamination from relations with other castes in general is the concern of a superior caste in relationship to an inferior one. But at times, even inferior castes are deeply resentful of being polluted by relationships with superior ones. It has been known, for example, that members of outcaste groups have punished even brahmins who have strayed into their living quarters.

The fourfold division of society into castes has been and is more of a theory than a reality. The theory, supported by such teachings as the Laws of Manu, was that almost everyone fell into one of the four castes. Of course, there were the *mlechchhas,* or foreigners. They were not Hindus in the first place. They did not acknowledge the Vedas, the validity of the brahminical system, and the other attributes of Hinduism. The foreigners were essentially barbarians who were beneath the dignity of even the *shudras.* In early times the *mlechchhas* included the Greeks and Persians, among others, and in later times included Muslims and Europeans. These had no place in the caste system.

Those persons and groups that did not fit into the fourfold caste system were designated as members of the *panchama,* or fifth caste. In actuality, however, considerable resistance to the use of

Friends and relatives sing from the Veda at a sacred thread ceremony.

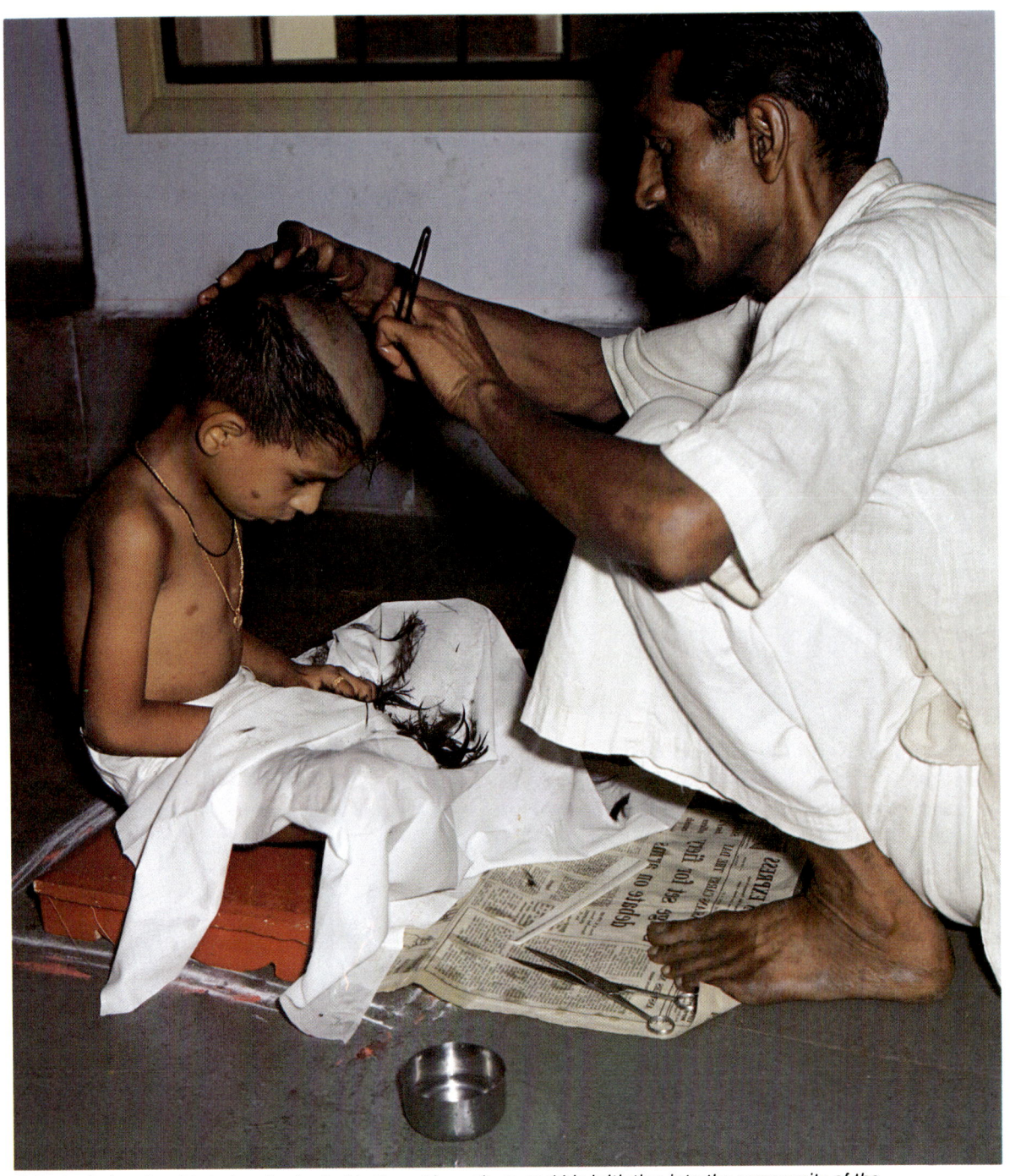

A Brahmin boy has his hair cut prior to his thread investiture and his initiation into the community of the twice-born.

this designation has existed because it seems to infer that in reality there are five rather than four castes. The pious Hindu would deny this, insisting that there can be only four. Other terms, then, have been employed to refer to the *panchamas,* such as outcastes, untouchables, depressed classes, and scheduled castes.

The *panchamas* include more than barbarians. They also consist of a number of tribes that usually are not of Aryan descent. These tribes often are still primitive and inhabit various unsettled areas in India. Often they take their names from their place of habitation and are associated with particular means of subsistence, such as hunting or coconut-growing. A few are not primitive and have developed considerable pride in themselves as well as worthwhile cultural contributions. In Vedic times one of the principal groups was the *candala,* which included members of more than one tribe. The *candalas* were required to live outside the villages. They also were required to make a loud sound whenever they entered the villages so that their presence could be known and they could be avoided by the caste Hindus. The *candalas* made their living chiefly by caring for corpses and by being public executioners. They wore the clothes of the dead, ate from broken vessels, and wore ornamentations only of iron.

The *panchamas* came about in other ways. In part they belonged to what has been called the criminal tribes, or castes, who made their living from unsanctioned activities. These were further subdivided into groups or subcastes that subsisted by theft and robbery, by fortune-telling and quackery, or by ritual killing. One such group, the Thugges, from whence comes the English word for thug, was a secret society whose members robbed and strangled their victims as a religious sacrifice to the goddess Bhavani, who is a form of the goddess Kali. The [British] in the last part of the nineteenth century were able to eliminate them [the Thugges] by taking drastic measures, including open violence. As a result of these and other reasons, the *panchamas* constitute a very large sector of the Indian population.

The *panchamas* are lowly and despised. No part of the Hinduism of the caste system pertains to them. They are not eligible to study the Vedas or to engage in rituals; they are even denied the right to perform the *sraddha* rituals for the benefit of their ancestors. They are forbidden to live near the members of the accepted castes, and under no circumstances may they touch members of the four castes. They are, for practical purposes, regarded almost as subhuman and they live often on an essentially animal level. The constitution of democratic India, however, has forbidden any discrimination against the *panchamas* and indeed has taken measures to uplift them. But it must be said that socially derived distinctions are very slow to change even when they are annulled by formal documents and intentions. The Hindu scriptures speak of the *panchamas* as *avarna,* or casteless, and such many of them are even today. Nongovernmental efforts to modify the caste system, including that of the status of the *panchamas,* have characterized the modern period of Hinduism's development. Several reformers have made significant contributions. The westernization of India's life, including the travel and study of Indians abroad, also has been potent. These influences have made some headway, it is true, but there seems to be no well-founded set of reasons for supposing that the main features of the caste system will soon be eliminated. One of the chief influences for the maintenance of the system is Hinduism itself.

"Untouchable" women in a village in Uttar Pradesh.

Students sit on the lawn of Visva-Bharati University, founded in 1924 by the poet Rabindranath Tagore.

READING 7
The Stages of Life*
FLOYD H. ROSS and TYNETTE HILLS

The ancient Hindus knew that there were certain periods in a person's life when one goal could be more easily sought than at other times. They divided life into several stages, and then they tried to point out what pleasures or actions were appropriate for each stage. Instruction in the four goals was to be given according to the individual's readiness to learn about them and his ability to achieve them at that time.

For example, the child does not need to worry about his later economic and ethical obligations to society. He will have time to learn about them as he grows older. Neither is a child ready for an adult religious experience. Therefore, it would be foolish to expect him to achieve those adult goals. Persons whose duty to caste codes requires them to devote a great deal of time and effort to economic activity are not expected to be very concerned about that most important goal of union of *Atman* and *Brahman*. This is true of the lowest caste group, the workers. However, Indians have never claimed the members of the lowest caste cannot realize such a union in their present lifetimes. It simply is not expected of them, because they are required to be so busy with other responsibilities.

All male members of the three higher castes are advised to follow the suggested life plan, whereby they might attain all the

*Adapted from Floyd H. Ross and Tynette Hills, *The Great Religions By Which Men Live* (Greenwich, Conn.: Fawcett Publications, 1956), pp. 35–39.

goals. The ancient teachers who developed the plan emphasized the importance of studying and interpreting life. In following the plan, a man will become in successive stages a student, a householder, a retired man, and a spiritual pilgrim.

THE STUDENT STAGE

The length of time spent in this stage varies, depending upon the particular caste to which one belongs. Every young man of the upper castes is expected to live for a time with his religious tutor who teaches him the ancient wisdom of India and directs his reading of the sacred books. Each student is personally helped to learn the meaning of life and is encouraged to find his proper place in it.

According to tradition, no young man in the student phase of his life is supposed to marry. In modern India, however, many of the old customs are not followed as strictly as formerly. Today, some marriages do occur before the young man has completed the usual student phase—but they are comparatively few in number. Many Indian parents still choose the wives for their sons. Since the arrangements are made by the parents of the couple, usually when they are both quite young, the young man is not expected to take time from his studies to court his future wife.

In general, there is no social custom comparable to the dating done in the United States today. The adults do not pretend that young people are not interested in the opposite sex. They simply arrange that the interest will not be unduly aroused before the young people are ready for the responsibilities of children. For the three higher castes, this usually means after the young men have passed through the student phases of their lives. Indian law now requires that a girl must be at least fifteen years of age before she can marry; the boy may not be married before eighteen.

There are reasons why the student stage is important enough to be completed. Every person has a natural capacity to wonder about life and to raise questions about it. Many of those questions are so big that no person has ever found more than a partial answer, but people seem somehow driven to keep trying to find answers, to learn and continue to learn. The student stage promotes this learning process.

According to Hindus, it also gives one a chance to get what they call his "second birth." The first birth was an event over which one had no control, but the second birth is in part an achievement resulting from one's own efforts. The Indians call it a spiritual rebirth: a young person begins to see something of the meaning of life. It is essential that one catch the meaning of life before he assumes family obligations.

THE HOUSEHOLDER STAGE

Although one should retain the student's desire to learn, he cannot remain forever with a teacher. Soon the former student is expected to marry and undertake the responsibilities of parenthood. In the householder stage, the Hindu can attain three of the four goals of life. He can find the meaning of the life of pleasure, for the marriage relationship should help to release all the basic human energies and drives. Being a member of the family requires that the person make his own contribution to the economic stability of society by productive work. And certainly the householder has opportunities to do his duty according to the ethical code of his caste. If India has changed slowly through the years, it is because of the specific rights and duties that were regarded as binding on each person in each caste.

THE RETIRED STAGE

The three goals that can be attained in the householder stage of life are important. But they should contribute to a larger goal—the finding of the real self and the real nature of the universe. Therefore, the Hindus provided for a third step, retirement from public life, at which time a man (and his wife with him, if they so wish it) might return to student interests. After one's first grandchild is born, one is permitted to withdraw from business or professional activities, give up direct family responsibilities, and retire to a forest hermitage for study. In a group of like-minded retired persons, the middle-aged student now has the opportunity to push further than in his student days the questions: What is the meaning of life? What am I? What is God like?

Not everyone in India can go on to this stage. Members of the upper castes normally have a better chance to do so because of the more favorable economic conditions which are theirs. People in India live in large family groups instead of in single-family units as Americans usually do. If one man leaves the large family compound, he is not missed as badly as he would be in a single family plan. Even in America, some people retire from business after the children are married. In India, a man who retires does so not only from business but also from the usual daily activities of the householder or family stage. He has outgrown the need for the earlier kinds of amusement and activities. He wants to reflect, to study, to meditate.

THE STAGE OF SPIRITUAL PILGRIM

There is a fourth stage that can be undertaken—but few enter into it. If he feels ready to do so, a man may leave his hermitage, his village, his group of congenial friends. Taking his staff and begging bowl, he wanders from place to place without cares or worries—eating whatever comes his way through the grace of those dwelling in the villages through which he travels. He helps the people by sharing his wisdom about the meaning of life or merely by his presence. He may live for a while as the tutor of a young student; but when he finishes the task, he wanders off again.

Westerners have frequently scorned this ideal. Yet, as Indians who know the story of Jesus point out, Jesus was demanding something like this of his own immediate followers. They were to give up everything—including family obligations—in order to follow him. To those who were ready for the step, he gave the invitation: leave everything. The search for meaning is more important than any institution—even the family. The wandering Hindu pilgrim is expressing this conviction dramatically when he leaves every vestige of his former life, in full dedication to the attempt to understand the real self. The attempt may result in physical hardship and loneliness, but the Hindu pilgrim believes these to be unimportant, for the *Atman* lies beyond comfort and companionship.

Hinduism teaches that people can find the real self only if they search honestly. The search starts during their student days. It goes on through their family days and their retired days. The search does not involve giving up anything that is natural. One should not try to repress or suppress part of his life, his feelings, or his emotions. One should try to see all the desires, urges, and feelings for what they are.

Pilgrims come from all over India to bathe in the sacred Ganges River.

Facing these honestly, a person discovers many things about himself. When he discovers what he himself is, he discovers what he is most capable of doing. Doing that with all of his heart just because he wants to do it, and doing it with love, he discovers that he is worshiping. To worship God is at the same time to find the real self and its meaning. These values are to be found only by the person who, with the honest desire to learn the answers to his basic questions, plans and lives his life for fulfillment of his highest goals.

READING 8
The Role of Women in Hinduism*
KENNETH W. MORGAN

The role of woman in Hinduism is closely associated with the life of the family. In all the religious practices and social duties of a householder he can count on the willing cooperation and help of his wife. A man's religious life is considered to be essentially deficient without his wife's active participation in it. Certain ceremonies cannot be performed by a Brahmin unless his wife is with him.

From the ultimate philosophical point of view there is no difference between man and woman, and what has been said about the distinction between the essential self and the empirical self of man, his karma and rebirths and his ultimate goal of liberation, is equally applicable to woman. Limitations are found primarily in religious and social fields, largely concerned with details rather than the spirit of religious practice. Some of the special sacraments do not apply to women and others are performed without the accompaniment of sacred mantras. A woman is not entitled to the rite of initiation at which the man is invested with the sacred thread and initiated into the responsibilities of his life as a student. The most important sacrament for a woman is marriage. After marriage a woman is generally considered to have no existence apart from her husband, especially so far as religious practices are concerned. Her husband is her

*Adapted from Kenneth W. Morgan, ed., *The Religion of the Hindus: Interpreted by Hindus* (New York: Ronald Press, 1953), pp. 140–41.

proper spiritual preceptor, or guru, and in all spiritual matters she is dependent on him. The conscientious performance of household duties constitutes her proper ritual. In popular Hinduism, however, greater freedom is allowed women in the matter of worship and other religious practices.

Contradictory views have been expressed concerning the social status of a Hindu woman. On the one hand she is said to be deserving of worship and respect, and on the other we are told in the Laws of Manu that "Father protects her in childhood, husband in youth, and sons in old age; a woman does not deserve to remain free." That contradiction is more apparent than real, for the emphasis is not on the denial of woman's freedom, but on the duty of her near relatives to protect her at all costs, for woman is indeed too precious a treasure of mankind to be neglected or treated lightly. It must, however, be added that the legal implications of that passage have not been at all favorable to the woman.

. . .It is indeed well and truly said that, for the Hindu, a home is not really a home unless a woman presides over it. In her role as the mistress of the house she is responsible for the solidarity and stability of the family. Without a wife, according to the scriptures, the psychological and moral personality of man remains imperfect. She is his constant companion in his religious life, preparing for him the sacred articles used in worship, accompanying him on pilgrimages, present at all ceremonies. Kalidasa[1] may be said to have epitomized beautifully the ideal of a Hindu wife when he characterized her as mistress of the home, counselor, friend of intimate moments, and beloved pupil in all the fine arts. And finally, in her role as the mother, woman is regarded as divine, respected many times more than the father and the teacher. Indeed there could not have been a higher compliment paid to a mother than the stirring words which are credited to Sankara,[2] "A bad son may be born, but there never is a bad mother."

Hindu bride and groom. Marriages are generally arranged by the parents of the couple.

---

[1] Sanskrit poet and dramatist (fifth century A.D.).
[2] Hindu philospher (eighth century A.D.).

READING 9
The Paths*
AINSLIE T. EMBREE

INTRODUCTION

One of the most important features of the religious life was the rise of sects or cults which have remained an essential feature of Hinduism. These sects were marked by two features which were of great significance for the spiritual life of India. One was *bhakti,* an attitude of devotion and adoration towards some particular god. The other was an emphasis on the grace of this deity in freely granting salvation to his devotees. The deities that were the object of devotion seem, in general, to have been of two kinds: either folk heroes who were deified (or, conceivably, deities who were made culture heroes), or personifications of some natural force. Krishna and Rama are examples of the first class, Shiva of the second, although Krishna and Rama are not strictly comparable to Shiva, since they are regarded as incarnations of Vishnu. In any case, it is around Vishnu, in one of his incarnations, or Shiva that the sectarian cults are mainly centered. Both deities were widely worshipped in some form by about 300 A.D., and it is quite possible that by then most of the people would have classed themselves as followers of one or the other. Thus the distinction between the Vaishnavite, or follower of Vishnu, and the Shaivite, became a basic feature of Hinduism.

---

*Adapted from Ainslie T. Embree, ed., *The Hindu Tradition* (New York: Random House, Vintage Books, 1966), pp. 117-29, 194-97.

The devotees of Vishnu picture their deity, either in his own person or in that of his incarnations, as beneficent and loving. Symbols denoting light and the life-giving sun are frequently associated with him, and his grace in offering salvation to his followers is stressed. This aspect of the Vishnu cult is prominent in the *Bhagavad Gita,* the greatest literary monument of the cults that emphasized worship of an individual god. This famous work forms a part of the *Mahabharata,* but is probably a separate composition. It exalts Krishna as supreme deity, but endeavors to bring all of the main trends of religious experience into a harmonious whole. Partly because it offers something to seekers of all kinds, partly because it synthesizes the ethical and religious insights of the Hindu tradition into a coherent statement, the *Gita* has played an important role in the life of India.

Shiva is almost certainly one of the most ancient of Indian gods, dating back before the physical and spiritual conquest of India by the Aryans. Images found at the sites of the prehistoric Indus Valley civilization bear a striking resemblance to later representations of Shiva, and his cult is strongest in South India, the area where Aryan influences were latest in coming. He is a god of fertility and power, but he is also pictured as an ascetic, covered with ashes and with snakes garlanded around his neck. Most frequently worshipped through a phallic symbol, a reminder of his origin as a god of fertility, he is also the Lord of the Dance, maintaining the cosmic order through his energy and power.

A characteristic feature of the Hindu tradition, the use of images in worship, is associated with the rise to prominence of the great cults. Images of the gods seem to have been unknown in Vedic times, but probably the emphasis on devotion offered to one particular deity fostered the use of plastic [sculptured] representations. Whatever the cause, images of all kinds became one of the most obvious marks of Hinduism, with carving becoming one of the most highly developed of the arts. The religious life of the people was thus nourished on a visual statement unmatched, perhaps, in the history of any civilization.

The Buddhist and Jain movements which flourished in the centuries when Vaishnavism and Shaivism were also taking hold can only be mentioned in passing, although they influenced the Hindu tradition at many points. The intermixing of the various movements was an extremely complex process, which, because of the lack of detailed historical data, cannot be analyzed with any certainty. The use of images in Buddhism, for example, might seem to be a clear case of the influence of the sectarian cults, but the very widespread and early use of images by Buddhism suggests the possiblity that the influence was the other way around.

MAN'S TRUE NATURE

For Indian religion salvation is understood in terms of the fundamental beliefs in *karma* and rebirth. On one level, the search for salvation is related to an attempt to improve one's *karma,* the fruit of one's actions, in order to improve one's future existence. On another and higher level, salvation is understood as the finding of a mode of existence that is beyond the changing flux of time and circumstance. This concept was directly linked to the ancient message of the *Upanishads* that there is an identity between man's spirit and the universal spirit, and that salvation consisted in an intuitive realization of this truth. To come to this state of knowledge is to realize man's true nature.

A description of man's nature is placed near the beginning of the *Bhagavad Gita,* where Arjuna, the great warrior, is filled with horror at the consequences that will follow from the fratricidal war in which he is engaged. Krishna, who is acting as his charioteer, insists that the first prerequisite for facing this and all other problems is an understanding of the true nature of human existence. Krishna's statement is one of the *Bhagavad Gita's* most famous passages.

> The Blessed Lord said:
> You grieve for those who should not be mourned, and yet you speak words of wisdom! The learned do not grieve for the dead or for the living.
> Never, indeed, was there a time when I was not, nor when you were not, nor these lords of men. Never, too, will there be a time, hereafter, when we shall not be.
> As in this body, there are for the embodied one [i.e., the soul] childhood, youth, and old age, even so there is the taking on of another body. The wise sage is not perplexed thereby.
> Contacts of the sense-organs, O son of Kunti, give rise to cold and heat, and pleasure and pain. They come and go, and are not permanent. Bear with them, O Bharata.

That man, whom these [sense-contacts] do not trouble, O chief of men, to whom pleasure and pain are alike, who is wise—he becomes eligible for immortality.

For the nonexistent there is no coming into existence; nor is there passing into nonexistence for the existent. The ultimate nature of these two is perceived by the seers of truth.

Know that to be indestructible by which all this is pervaded. Of this imperishable one, no one can bring about destruction.

These bodies of the eternal embodied one, who is indestructible and incomprehensible, are said to have an end. Therefore fight, O Bharata.

He who regards him [i.e., the soul] as a slayer, and he who regards him as slain—both of them do not know the truth; for this one neither slays nor is slain.

He is not born, nor does he die at any time; nor, having once come to be will he again come not to be. He is unborn, eternal, permanent, and primeval; he is not slain when the body is slain.

Whoever knows him to be indestructible and eternal, unborn and immutable [constant]—how and whom can such a man, O son of Pritha, cause to be slain or slay?

Just as a man, having cast off old garments, puts on other, new ones, even so does the embodied one, having cast off old bodies, take on other, new ones.

Weapons do not cleave him, fire does not burn him; nor does water drench him, nor the wind dry him up.

He is uncleavable, he is unburnable, he is undrenchable, as also undryable. He is eternal, all-pervading, stable, immovable, existing from time immemorial.

He is said to be unmanifest, unthinkable, and unchangeable. Therefore, knowing him as such, you should not grieve [for him]. And even if you regard him as being perpetually born and as perpetually dying, even then, O long-armed one, you should not grieve for him.

For, to one who is born death is certain and certain is birth to one who has died. Therefore in connection with a thing that is inevitable you should not grieve. . . .

Unmanifest in their beginnings are beings, manifest in the middle stage, O Bharata, and unmanifest, again, in their ends. For what then should there be any lamentation [expression of grief]?

Someone perceives him as a marvel; similarly, another speaks of him as a marvel; another, again, hears of him as a marvel; and, even after hearing of him, no one knows him.

Women in traditional Indian dress celebrate the birthday of Lord Krishna.

> The embodied one within the body of everyone, O Bharata, is ever unslayable. Therefore, you should not grieve for any being. . . .
> When one renounces all the desires which have arisen in the mind, O son of Pritha, and when he himself is content within his own Self, then is he called a man of steadfast wisdom.
> He whose mind is unperturbed in the midst of sorrows and who entertains no desires amid pleasure; he from whom passion, fear, and anger have fled away—he is called a sage of steadfast intellect.
> He who feels no attachment toward anything; who, having encountered the various good or evil things, neither rejoices nor loathes—his wisdom is steadfast.
> When one draws in, on every side, the sense-organs from the objects of sense as a tortoise draws in its limbs from every side—then his wisdom becomes steadfast.[1]

A. The Way of Salvation: Duty

Having stated the goal, Krishna proceeds to show how it may be obtained. His definition of the end of life as a state beyond any attachment, including concern for the results of action, raises the problem of how action can be performed without motivation, that is, without being involved in its result. He gives the answer in terms of performance of *dharma,* the duties appropriate to one's particular class. This fulfillment of one's obligations as defined by life is known as *karma yoga,* the discipline of action, but it must be carefully distinguished from what is known in western thought as "salvation by works." *Karma yoga,* the way of obedience to the demands imposed by a particular existence, is a necessity for all those who seek to escape from the involvement in the fruits of actions, or, in other words, in rebirth.

> Not by nonperformance of actions does a man attain freedom from action; nor by mere renunciation of actions does he attain his spiritual goal.
> For no one, indeed, can remain, for even a single moment, unengaged in activity, since everyone, being powerless, is made to act by the dispositions of matter.
> Whoever having restrained his organs of action still continues to brood over the objects of senses—he, the deluded one, is called a hypocrite.

---

[1] From *Bhagavad Gita,* II:11–30, 55–59, in *Sources of Indian Tradition,* ed. by William T. de Bary et al. (New York: Columbia University Press, 1958), pp. 284–85, 298.

But he who, having controlled the sense-organs by means of the mind, O Arjuna, follows without attachment the path of action by means of the organs of action—he excels.

Do your allotted work, for action is superior to nonaction. Even the normal functioning of your body cannot be accomplished through actionlessness.

Except for the action done for sacrifice, all men are under the bondage of action. Therefore, O son of Kunti, do you undertake action for that purpose, becoming free from all attachment. . . .

But the man whose delight is in the Self alone, who is content with the Self, who is satisfied only within the Self—for him there exists nothing that needs to be done.

He, verily, has in this world no purpose to be served by action done nor any purpose whatsoever to be served by action abnegated [denied]. Similarly, he does not depend on any beings for having his purpose served.

Therefore, without attachment, always do the work that has to be done, for a man doing his work without attachment attains to the highest goal. . . .

Better is one's own dharma [class duties] which one may be able to fulfill but imperfectly, than the dharma of others which is more easily accomplished. Better is death in the fulfillment of one's own dharma. To adopt the dharma of others is perilous. . . .

The fourfold class system was created by Me in accordance with the varying dispositions and the actions [resulting from them]. Though I am its creator, know Me, who am immutable, to be a non-doer.

Actions do not cling to Me, for I have no yearning for their fruit. He who knows Me thus [and himself acts in that spirit] is not bound by actions.

So knowing was action done even by men of old who sought liberation. Therefore do the same action [i.e., your class duties] which was done by the ancients in ancient times.

What is action? What is inaction?—as to this even the wise sages are confounded. I will expound action to you, knowing which you will be liberated from evil.

One has to realize what is action; similarly, one has to realize what is wrong action; and one has also to realize what is inaction. Inscrutable, indeed, is the way of action.

He who sees inaction in action and action in inaction, he is discerning among men, expert in the technique of karma-yoga, the doer of the entire action [enjoined by his dharma].

He whose undertakings are all devoid of motivating desires and purposes and whose actions are consumed by the fire of knowledge—him the wise call a man of learning.

Renouncing all attachment to the fruits of action, ever content, independent—such a person even if engaged in action, does not do anything whatever.[2]

B. The Way of Salvation: Knowledge

The second way commended by Krishna for a realization of the true nature of man is the path of knowledge. This does not mean the gaining of information or even of wisdom—although it includes knowledge of the scriptures and the teachings of the sages—but rather the acquisition of truth that comes through meditation. In the following selection both the fruits and techniques of this way, or *yoga,* are strikingly delineated.

To him who has subjugated [conquered] his self by his self, his self is a friend; but to him who has not restrained his self, his own self behaves inimically [hostilely], like an enemy. The self of one who has subjugated his self and is tranquil, is absolutely concentrated on itself, in the midst of cold and heat, pleasure and pain, as well as honour and dishonour. The devotee whose self is contented with knowledge and experience, who is unmoved, who has restrained his senses, and to whom a sod, a stone, and gold are alike, is said to be devoted. And he is esteemed highest, who thinks alike about well-wishers, friends, and enemies, and those who are indifferent, and those who take part with both sides, and those who are objects of hatred, and relatives, as well as about the good and the sinful. A devotee should constantly devote his self to abstraction, remaining in a secret place, alone, with his mind and self restrained, without expectations, and without belongings. Fixing his seat firmly in a clean place, not too high nor too low, and covered over with a sheet of cloth, a deerskin, and blades of Kusa grass—and there seated on that seat, fixing his mind exclusively on one point, with the workings of the mind and senses restrained, he should practice devotion for purity of self. Holding his body, head, and neck even and unmoved, remaining steady, looking at the tip of his own nose, and not looking about in all directions, with a tranquil self, devoid of fear, and adhering to the rules of chastity, he should restrain his mind, and concentrate it on me, and sit down engaged in devotion, regarding me as his final goal. Thus constantly devoting his self to abstraction, a devotee whose mind is restrained, attains that

[2]From *Bhagavad Gita,* III:3–9, 17–19, IV:13–20, in *Sources of Indian Tradition,* pp. 286–87, 289.

tranquillity which culminates in final emancipation, and assimilation with me. Devotion is not his, O Arjuna! who eats too much, nor his who eats not at all; not his who is addicted to too much sleep, nor his who is ever awake. That devotion which destroys all misery is his, who takes due food and exercise, who toils duly in all works, and who sleeps and awakes in due time. When a man's mind well restrained becomes steady upon the self alone, then he being indifferent to all objects of desire, is said to be devoted. As a light standing in a windless place flickers not, that is declared to be the parallel for a devotee, whose mind is restrained, and who devotes his self to abstraction.[3]

C. The Way of Salvation: Devotion

Throughout all the discussions of the ways of salvation in the *Bhagavad Gita* is the implicit assumption that transcending and completing the disciplines of work and knowledge is the way of devotion to Krishna as Supreme Lord. Through surrender to him, men find the final end they seek—the realization of their true self. It is this emphasis on devotion that has made the *Gita* the scripture that appeals most directly to the heart of the Indian people. The verses given here describe the glorious vision of Krishna that comes to Arjuna, overwhelming his senses with the splendor and power of the god who has sought through his love and mercy to bring him to a realization of the truth.

ARJUNA:
    Fain would I see,
As thou Thyself declar'st it, Sovereign Lord!
The likeness of that glory of Thy Form
Wholly revealed. O Thou Divinest One!
If this can be, if I may bear the sight,
Make Thyself visible, Lord of all prayers!
Show me Thy very self, the Eternal God!

KRISHNA:
Gaze, then, thou Son of Pritha! I manifest for thee
Those hundred thousand thousand shapes that clothe my Mystery:
I show thee all my semblances, infinite, rich, divine,
My changeful hues, my countless forms. See! in this face of mine . . .
Wonders unnumbered, Indian Prince! revealed to none save thee.
Behold! this is the Universe!—Look! what is live and dead

The worship of deities in shrines and temples is a vital Hindu tradition. Here a woman is worshipping Shiva.

[3]From *Bhagavad Gita*, VI:7-19, trans. by K. T. Telang in *Sacred Books of the East,* vol. VIII (Oxford: Clarendon Press, 1882), pp. 68-69.

I gather all in one—in Me! Gaze, as thy lips have said,
On GOD ETERNAL, VERY GOD! SEE ME! see what thou prayest!

* * * * * * * * * * * * *

Thou canst not!—nor, with human eyes, Arjuna! ever mayest!
Therefore I give thee sense divine. Have other eyes, new light!
And, look! This is My glory, unveiled to mortal sight!

ARJUNA:
      I mark Thee strike the skies
      With front in wondrous wise
Huge, rainbow-painted, glittering; and thy mouth
      Opened, and orbs which see
      All things whatever be,
In all Thy worlds, east, west, and north and south.
      O Eyes of God! O Head!
      My strength of soul is fled,
Gone is heart's force, rebuked is mind's desire!
      When I behold Thee so,
      With awful brows a-glow,
With burning glance, and lips lighted with fire,
      Fierce as those flames which shall
      Consume, at close of all.
Earth, Heaven! Ah me! I see no Earth and Heaven!
      Thee, Lord of Lords! I see,
      Thee only—only Thee!
Ah! let Thy mercy unto me given! . . .
      How, in the wide worlds three
      Should any equal be?
Shall any other share Thy majesty?
      Therefore, with body bent
      And reverent intent,
I praise, and serve, and seek Thee, asking grace.
      As father to a son,
      As friend to friend, as one
Who loveth to his lover, turn Thy face
      In gentleness on me!
      Good is it I did see
This unknown marvel of Thy Form! But fear
      Mingles with joy! Retake,
      Dear Lord! for pity's sake
Thine earthly shape, which earthly eyes may bear!

>   Be merciful, and show
>   The visage that I know;
> Let me regard Thee, as of yore, arrayed
>   With disc and forehead-gem,
>   With mace [staff] and anadem [head wreath],
> Thou who sustainest all things! Undismayed
>   Let me once more behold
>   The form I loved of old,
> Thou of the thousand arms and countless eyes!
>   My frightened heart is fain
>   To see restored again,
> The Charioteer, my Krishna's kind disguise....
>
> KRISHNA:
>   Yea! it was wonderful and terrible
>   To view me as thou didst, dear Prince! The gods
>   Dread and desire continually to view!
>   Yet not by Vedas, nor from sacrifice,
>   Nor penance, nor gift-giving, nor with prayer
>   Shall any so behold, as thou hast seen!
>   Only by fullest service, perfect faith,
>   And uttermost surrender am I known
>   And seen, and entered into, Indian Prince!
>   Who doeth all for Me; who findeth Me
>   In all; adoreth always; loveth all
>   Which I have made, and Me, for Love's sole end,
>   That man, Arjuna! unto Me doth wend.[4]

D. The Way of Discipline: Yoga[5]

Yoga is one of the most familiar of Indian religious terms, but its fame has tended to mask the real nature of its position. In the present context "disciplined activity" seems to give the sense intended by its usage in the basic text of the school, the *Yogasutra* of Patanjali. The dates of this work are quite uncertain, with some scholars assigning it to the second century B.C., and others to the fourth century A.D., but the surviving commentaries all seem to come from a time subsequent to the later date.

According to Patanjali, the aim of Yoga is to gain control of both physical and mental processes.... The yogic practitioner seeks through a careful process of spiritual exercises to reach a state of

---

[4]From *Bhagavad Gita,* XI, selected verses, trans. by Sir Edwin Arnold in *The Song Celestial* (Boston: Roberts, 1885).
[5]Some scholars classify Yoga as a way of salvation.

"isolation," of the complete separation of spirit from matter. When this is achieved the spirit is free from change and motion.

This selection describes the methods to be followed by the disciple, and while they are expressed in the telegraphic language common to the sutra form, their meaning is relatively clear.

1. Purificatory action [action serving to purify], study, and making God the motive of action, constitute the *yoga* of action.
2. This is for the bringing about of trance and for the purpose of attenuating [reducing] afflictions.
3. The afflictions are ignorance, egoism, attachment, aversion, and love of life.
4. Ignorance is the field for the others, whether dormant, tenuous [weak], alternated, or fully operative.
5. Ignorance is the taking of the temporal, the impure, the painful, and the not-self to be the eternal, the pure, the pleasurable, and the self.
6. Egoism is the belief that the power of seeing and the power by which one sees is a single essence.
7. Attachment is the attraction to pleasure.
8. Aversion is the repulsion from pain.
9. Flowing on by its own potency, established even in the wise, is love of life.
10. These afflictions may be overcome by their opposites.
11. Their activities are destroyed by meditation.
12. The vehicle of actions has its origin in afflictions, and is experienced in visible and invisible births.
13. It ripens into life-state, life-time, and life-experience, if the root exists.
14. They have pleasure or pain as the fruit, by reason of virtue or vice.
15. By reason of the pains of change, anxiety, and habituation, and by reason of the contrariety [the quality of being contrary] of the functionings of the "qualities," all indeed is pain to the discriminating.
16. But future pain is avoidable.
17. The conjunction of the knower and the knowable is the cause of avoidable pain. . . .
23. Conjunction is that which brings about the recognition of the natures of the power of owning and the capacity of being owned.

A yoga exercise—the sarvangasana *posture.*

24. Ignorance is its effective cause.
25. Removal (of bondage) is the disappearance of conjunction on account of the disappearance of ignorance, and that is the absolute freedom of the knower.
26. The means of removing ignorance is through knowledge that discriminates between the soul and the objects of sense. . . .
28. On the destruction of impurity by the sustained practice of the accessories of *yoga,* the light of wisdom reaches up to discriminative knowledge.
29. Restraint, observance, posture, regulation of breath, abstraction (of the senses), concentration, meditation, and trance are the eight accessories of *yoga.*
30. Of these, the restraints are: abstinence from injury *(ahimsa),* veracity [truthfulness], abstinence from theft, continence [self-restraint], and abstinence from avariciousness [greediness].
31. They are the great vow, universal, and unlimited by origin, space, time, and circumstance.
32. The observances are cleanliness, contentment, austerity, study, and the making of the Lord the motive of all action. . . .
35. In the presence of one who has given up causing injury, all hostility is given up.
36. When one is confirmed in veracity, actions and their consequences depend upon him.
37. When one is confirmed in the habit of not stealing, all treasures come to him.
38. Continence being confirmed, vigour is obtained.
39. Non-covetousness being confirmed, knowledge of the succession of births is obtained.
40. By cleanliness is meant disgust with one's body, and cessation of contact with others.
41. And with the mind becoming pure, come purity, singleness of mind, control of the senses, and fitness for the knowledge of the self.
42. By contentment, comes the acquisition of extreme happiness.
43. By purificatory action, come the removal of impurity and the attainments of the physical body and the senses.
44. By study comes communion with the desired deity.
45. The attainment of trance comes by making God the motive of all actions.
46. Posture is steady and easy. . . .
49. Regulation of breath is the stoppage of the inhaling and exhaling movements of breath. . . .

53. Then the mind is fit for concentration.
54. Abstraction (of the senses) is that by which the senses do not come into contact with their objects and follow as it were the nature of the mind.
55. Thence the senses are under the highest control.[6]

[6]From Patanjali, *Yogasutra,* Chapter II, trans. by Rama Prasad in *Sacred Books of the Hindus,* vol. IV, revised (Allahabad: Panini Office, 1924).

READING 10
Stories, Festivals, and Devotion*
PAUL YOUNGER and SUSANNA OOMMEN YOUNGER

Writers often try to make Hinduism look as much like a Western religion as possible. They therefore select from the great mass of material only those elements which seem to be theological or philosophical in character. Then with the help of historical imagination, they attempt to string those elements together to make a tradition. As a result, the actual content of the religious life of ordinary people is often ignored.

This section describes some of the content of the religious life of the ordinary people as it is expressed in the stories, festivals, and ceremonies through which they communicate with one another in their homes and villages. Some of the stories may seem quite simple; the festivals may appear to be nothing more than unsophisticated people having a good time; and even the ceremonies may seem old-fashioned. Indians think of the stories, festivals, ceremonies, and private patterns of devotion as part of the ever-changing scene of life, and there is no single pattern that is more sacred than all others. Every family, caste, or village has its own set of stories, festivals, and ceremonies. It would be impossible to describe them all, so the authors must subjectively choose certain ones in the hope of providing some insight into

---

*From Paul Younger and Susanna Oommen Younger, *Hinduism,* Major World Religion Series (Niles, Ill.: Argus Communications, 1978).

Hindu religious practices. What is important to understand is the fact that all Hindus are raised on a collection of stories, a number of enjoyable festivals, and a set of carefully observed ceremonies. Underlying these stories, festivals, and ceremonies are certain attitudes toward life which slowly and imperceptibly become a part of the personality of every Hindu, and indeed most Indians. . . .

STORIES

One of the greatest pleasures of Indian children is listening to stories. Most Indian homes are extended families, in that parents, grandparents, uncles, aunts, and cousins all live together. Indian children have many older people around to tell them stories. The immediate purpose of these stories may be to stir the emotions of children, but they also serve to teach them about the holy places of pilgrimage, great scholars, heroes or heroines, and the traditional Indian attitudes toward life. The following three stories are typical of those dear to Indian children.

The Mud Pie and the Dry Leaf

The Mud Pie and the Dry Leaf were great friends. As they were growing old they decided to make a pilgrimage to Banaras, the holy city on the banks of the Ganges River. They believed that if they washed themselves in the Ganges their sins would be erased. Being good friends, they discussed the distance they had to travel and the perils along the way. They agreed that heavy rains and gusts of wind would be the greatest hazards. So the Dry Leaf said he would cover his friend and shield him from danger if it rained, and the Mud Pie said he would do the same if there was a strong wind.

The two had gone some distance when the winds started blowing. The Mud Pie sat on his friend and saved him. A little later the rains came. Then the Dry Leaf covered his friend and saved him. The sun shone again, and the two friends resumed their journey. A few days later the clouds darkened the skies once again. Heavy rains were accompanied by strong gusts of wind. Although the friends tried their best to help each other, the Dry Leaf was blown away and the Mud Pie was washed away.

The Fable of Kanya Kumari[1]

There was a beautiful princess in this southern part of the country whose hand was sought in marriage by many valiant princes. Finally a handsome and noble prince was chosen to be the bridegroom. Great preparations were made for the wedding. The marriage feast, which consisted of many exotic dishes, was prepared by the best cooks of the land. Many different kinds of rice were cooked. The bride, bedecked with jewels, looked radiant in her lovely wedding *sari*. Everything was ready. But due to some unknown reason, the bridegroom failed to show up. Alas! Where there had been great rejoicing, there was now mourning and sadness. The great wedding feast went to waste. The remains turned into multicolored sand—sand resembling rice and sand resembling broken rice. The princess died of a broken heart soon after. Hence the place came to be called Kanya Kumari.

Panini[2]

When Panini was a young lad, an elderly man who was adept at palmistry took the boy's right hand and studied it carefully. After some time, he shook his head sadly. Panini was puzzled and asked what was wrong.

The old man said, "You are a fine lad. Your heart is sound. You have a good mind and your life line is not bad. But alas, there is absolutely nothing where a career line should be! You might end up as a nonentity and a dunce."

Panini thanked the old man for his kindness. Then he took a small knife and made a long, straight line where his career line should have been. After that he put his mind to his studies. He won great renown as a scholar, and modern scholars now look on him as the greatest of all Indian grammarians.

One famous collection of fables from ancient India is the *Panchatantra* (meaning "five parts"). It was probably compiled about 200 B.C. but contains many stories that are older. The stories in this collection were supposed to have been used by a Brahmin scholar who had to teach the three sons of a famous

Celebrants in the Holi Festival throw colored water and powder at each other.

---

[1] Kanya Kumari (virgin princess) is the southernmost point of India. It is a sacred place and has a beautiful shore temple. Both sunrise and sunset can be seen from the same vantage point. The sand on the seashore is multicolored and of an amazing variety.

[2] Panini was a Sanskrit scholar of antiquity. The word *pani* means "hand."

king. When he started teaching, he realized that the boys were not very bright. So he told these stories in order to help them learn something about how to deal with people and situations in life. It is not customary for Indians to attach morals to stories. They usually tell stories and hope the children will be inspired. In the case of the *Panchatantra,* however, a moral is tagged on to every tale. Here is one fable from this collection.

The Turtle Who Fell off a Stick

Near a certain lake there lived a turtle and two swans. They were good friends. One year there was a severe drought and the lake started to dry up. The three wondered how they could save themselves. Suddenly the turtle had a brilliant idea. He said, "First, find a lake full of water; then bring me a strong stick. I'll hold onto the middle of it by my mouth. You hold the ends and carry me to our new lake."

The birds agreed it was an excellent idea but warned him, "When we are flying, take care not to open your mouth!"

Finally the swans found the ideal lake and the stick and got ready for their flight. They had to fly over a city. People looked up in amazement and said, "Look at those clever birds carrying something. It is a turtle!"

The turtle heard this and started to say, "What is all this excitement about? Me?" Alas! He didn't and couldn't finish what he had to say.

Moral: Silence is golden.

FESTIVALS

There are all kinds of festivals in India. Some usher in a new season and others the New Year. Some are in celebration of the harvest season, which has a great significance in India where the majority of people are dependent on the land for sustenance. As festivals are observed according to the lunar and solar calendars, there is no single New Year's Day. The New Year is ushered in at different times in different places in India. Some festivals are in honor of gods or goddesses and others re-create the atmosphere of favorite stories from the *Mahabharata* or the *Ramayana.*

Holi

The Holi festival, which ushers in the spring (in March), is well known to tourists visiting India. It is celebrated primarily in the north and is associated with Kama, the god of love. It might remind a Westerner of a Mardi Gras or Halloween celebration; people throw colored water at each other and play practical jokes.

Kumbha Mela

There is a very special religious festival called Kumbha Mela. It is considered the world's greatest religious concourse and is held about every twelve years at four sacred places in northern India. The one at the city of Allahabad is the largest, with as many as ten million pilgrims assembling from all parts of the subcontinent. A cross section of Hindu India can be seen here—peasants, merchants, paupers, misers, moneylenders, pundits [scholars] and illiterates, naked holy men and the sophisticated elite. Kumbha Mela is celebrated when the sun and the moon are in Mesha (Aries) and Jupiter passes through Kumbha (Aquarius).

The Kumbha Mela is primarily a ritual bathing festival associated with Mother Ganga, or the holy river Ganges. Water from any part of the Ganges is considered sacred, but the stretch of river at Allahabad, where the Ganges and Jumna rivers join, is considered the most sacred.

Divali

Divali (or Dipavali) literally means "a garland of lights." It is considered the national festival of India since it is the most widely celebrated. This is a time when the darkness of misery and poverty is replaced by the radiance of innumerable lights. People don festive clothes. Sweets, usually made of thickened milk and sugar or with freshly grated coconut and sugar, are made and distributed lavishly. People in the wealthy mercantile communities of western India paint their houses, open new account books, start everything afresh. They pay homage to household deities, especially to Lakshmi, the goddess of wealth and good fortune.

This festival falls in the month of Kartik (October-November) and marks the beginning of the New Year for many. As the title implies, it is, above all, a festival of lights. After supper people go out to view the rows and rows of lights illuminating every household—tiny earthenware lamps with saucerlike depressions holding the oil and the wicks. The lamps burn throughout the night. It is a beautiful sight that defies description.

Fireworks are set off, to the great delight of children for whom Divali is, perhaps, the most joyous of all festivals. In Bengal, Divali illuminations take the form of lighted torches on long poles. Some believe that the torches serve as guiding lights for the souls of visiting departed ancestors.

The exact origin of Divali, like that of many Indian festivals, is shrouded in antiquity. Vaishnavites (those who worship Vishnu as the supreme deity) believe that Divali grew out of the magnificent celebrations connected with the coronation of Rama as the king of Ayodhya. According to the *Ramayana,* Sita, the beautiful wife of Rama, is rescued and enthroned beside him. She looks radiant in shining garments and jewelry. There is great rejoicing in Ayodhya, for the demon of darkness has been removed. The streets and houses of Ayodhya shine with the radiance of rows of lights. People who had been sorrowing long in the absence of their rightful king have donned their brightest clothing and celebrate by throwing flower petals in the air as symbols of gladness. Thus many look upon Divali as a colorful and joyful festival celebrating the happy ending of the epic *Ramayana.*

Onam

Divali is little celebrated in Kerala, chiefly because the Onam festival occurs there a few weeks earlier. (Celebrations are usually a drain on the family purse, and people are unable to indulge in them too often.) The Onam festival takes place early in the month of September in the midst of the harvest season. The torrential monsoons have stopped, and the crops are abundant. People wear and exchange new clothes, usually made of fine cotton with gold borders. Houses are cleaned and decorated. The prayer rooms are profusely decorated with flower petals, while courtyards are adorned with complicated geometrical designs made with rice flour mixed with water.

All sorts of vegetables grow in Kerala. Elaborate vegetarian dishes and different kinds of rice and yogurt preparations are served at the Onam feast. Bananas are a must for this festival.

A young woman in northern India lights the Divali Festival lamps.

Different varieties of plantains are grown in Kerala, but only one is called the banana. It is much bigger than the other plantains, has a different texture, and is rich in protein.

Women, their coiled hair decked with jasmine and roses, dance special Onam dances. Men indulge in vigorous sports. The famous boat race of Kerala is held at this time.

The festival is said to have originated as follows:

An *asura* (demon) king named Mahabali ruled in southern India (probably over what is now Tamil Nadu and Kerala). Unlike the typical *asura,* Mahabali followed the path of *dharma* and ruled over his people wisely and well. They in turn adored him. Under Mahabali's rule there was no shortage of any good thing; there was no theft or murder, neither famine nor pestilence, and all were equal.

The gods soon became jealous of Mahabali's popularity. They held council together and decided to send Vishnu to earth as Vamana, a mean and hungry-looking dwarf. Vamana approached Mahabali and asked of him a bit of land, as much as he could measure in three strides. Mahabali, noting Vamana's diminutive size, said he would be most happy to give him the land. At this, before the amazed eyes of onlookers, Vamana grew into a giant of immense proportions. He measured the whole of the earth in two strides and then asked Mahabali where he could place his foot for the third stride. Mahabali, recognizing Lord Vishnu, knelt in front of him and requested that the god place his foot on his head. Vamana stepped on Mahabali and pushed him down to the nether world.

Before he was banished thus, Mahabali asked for a favor—that he be allowed to visit his beloved people once a year. Vishnu granted his wish. The people of Kerala believe that Mahabali visits them at Onam time. Everybody tries to be joyous and happy so that when Mahabali comes he will be pleased.

Festival Deities

The following deities are especially celebrated in festivals.

Lakshmi, the consort of Vishnu, is worshiped widely as the goddess of beauty, wealth, and prosperity. The wife in the home is compared to Lakshmi—the symbol of light, prosperity, and good fortune. Although Kubera is the god of wealth and his fabled celestial abode sparkles with jewels, he is not considered worthy of worship because he is selfish, miserly, and interested only in amassing riches for himself.

Durga and Kali are worshiped widely, especially in Bengal. They are considered manifestations of Parvati (the consort of Shiva), who is the mother goddess—the symbol of strength and power. Durga is represented as having a gentle face and eight arms, each of which holds a weapon. Kali, on the other hand, is formidable and is represented as black and wearing a garland of skulls. She is said to have destroyed *kala* (time) itself.

Sarasvati, the consort of Brahma the creator, is the goddess of learning—the patroness of all the creative arts and sciences. She is represented as reclining on a swan or peacock with a *vina* (a type of musical instrument) in her hand. During Sarasvati Puja,[3] a festival in her honor, scholars, musicians, and artists all worship her. Books, pens, musical instruments, paintbrushes, paints, sculptor's tools—all of these are placed in front of her image for a day. Hindu school boys and girls eagerly look forward to this day of relaxation and recess from schoolwork.

Ganesha (or Ganapati), the son of Shiva, is the god who removes all obstacles. Hence his aid is invoked at the beginning of any important venture in life. Ganapati Puja is the most important of all festivals in Maharashtra.

Hanuman, the monkey god, is worshiped widely, especially in Gujarat, because of his devotion to Rama. His relentless efforts to find Sita and his superhuman acts of heroism make him a great favorite of all devotees of Lord Rama.

Music and Dance

In most of the festivals and ceremonies of India, music and dance play an important part. Music is used to express the tone or mood of a festival or ceremony. Different *ragas*[4] reflect the moods of joy, sadness, or excitement. In ceremonies or in dramas, which are so often part of a festival, it is the character of the music which establishes the mood of the participants. Many Westerners who

---

[3] *Puja* means "worship" or "homage."
[4] Traditional melodic patterns.

have come to appreciate Indian music may not be aware that much of its richness comes from the close way in which the music reflects the cycle or aspect of life it depicts.

Dance in India is not a social phenomenon but is usually a highly developed and sophisticated form of religious art. There is a rich variety: the joyful folk dances of the tribal people, the complex dramatic dances of religious festivals (*Kathakali* of Kerala being the best known), and the sophisticated abstract expression of *bharata natyam* (dance of India). One of the best known of the *bharata natyam* dances is the one which attempts to portray the ten *avataras* (incarnations) of Vishnu. The dances, while depicting religious themes, also portray the basic emotions of human experience through subtle movements of the dancer's body and by facial expressions. The most important forms of expression are those made with various movements and placements of the hands.

PATTERNS OF WORSHIP

Any discussion of the religious life of India must include the way Hindus worship. As religion is an intensely personal matter, there are many ways in which Hindus worship the deity of their choice. Some individuals go to temples daily, some less often; others go only on special occasions—holy days or festival days. Some seek special blessings and hence go when the need is felt. Whatever the occasion, everyone takes an offering to the deity—flowers, coconuts, ghee (clarified butter), sweets, and so forth. The priest will place the offering in front of the deity, then return part of it to the devotee. If the portions are plentiful and considered delectable, the devotee will distribute them to members of the family as well as to friends and relatives. The offering thus distributed is called *prasada,* which means it has the blessing of the deity.

People also go to temples to hear discourses. These usually occur in the early evening, and a *pundit* (learned man) will expound the scriptures to the usually predominantly female audience. Because the climate is warm, these religious discourses are often held in the temple grounds. Some of the texts expounded will be in Sanskrit, some in the local language. The

A Kathakali dancer. The dance, performed outdoors, lasts all night. Dancers are men and boys who play both men's and women's parts. Dance movements and gestures are vigorous and strong.

people who attend will mostly be simple folk. Some will listen with earnest attention while others, weary from the day's hard labor, will lean against the wall and doze. Passages from the *Bhagavad Gita* and Shankara's teachings are favored by the *pundits*. The people particularly enjoy passages written by the saints of their region.

Devotional passages such as these are often chosen:

> Worship the Lord, you fool! When the appointed time comes, repeating the fine rules of grammar will not avail you any. (From Shankara's hymn "Bhaja Govindam.")

> The letter A is the beginning of the alphabet; even so God is the first Cause of the world. Of what use is great learning if one does not worship Him who is possessed of pure Knowledge? (The opening lines of *Thirukkural*.[5])

A woman performs aarti—*the waving of a burning lamp—before Ganesha at her home shrine.*

---

[5] The "divine utterance" of a Tamil saint of the second century B.C.

The temple teaching is as much about right living as it is about devotion. Verses from the *dharma shastras* (sacred texts) are used in some parts of India. In Madras, verses from the *Thirukkural* are very popular:

> Those who desire the higher pleasures of heaven will not act unjustly through desire of the trifling joy of this life.
> To bear with those who revile us even as the earth bears up with those who dig it is the first of virtues.
> Forget anger toward everyone, as fountains of evil come from it.

Popular as temple worship may be, worship in the home is even more widely practiced. In most homes the prayer room is elaborately decorated and furnished with images of favorite deities on a raised dais. Pictures of gods and goddesses adorn the walls. (Even in humble homes the best wall is reserved for pictures of deities.) Five- or seven-wick oil lamps made of silver or brass are lighted at the time of prayer. Aside from morning worship, a simple *sandhya namaskaram* (dusk worship) is held.

The woman of the house is the one who is diligent about the prayer ceremony, although the householder usually takes a brief moment or two to pay homage before he leaves for work. The entire family participates in the prayer ceremony of special occasions—holy days, festival days, birthdays, anniversaries of deaths, at the start of a journey, on safe arrival from a distant land, when embarking on a special venture, after the wedding when the bride leaves the home with the groom, and so forth.

It is in these domestic ceremonies that much of the Hindu's religious life shows itself. Indeed, one can learn a great deal about Hinduism from books, but if one wishes to experience the religiousness of the Hindus, one must visit their homes.

> OM
> Filled with Brahman are the things we see,
> Filled with Brahman are the things we see not,
> From out of Brahman floweth all that is:
> From Brahman all—yet is he still the same.
> OM . . . Peace—peace—peace.
>
> Lead me from the unreal to the real.
> Lead me from darkness to light.
> Lead me from death to immortality.
>
> Opening lines of *Brihadaranyaka Upanishad*

Glossary

Definitions are limited to those that apply to usage of words and phrases within this volume. Italic words in the definitions are defined elsewhere in the Glossary.

Ahimsa. Noninjury to living things; reverence for all life.

Allahabad. A *Ganges River* city of northern India in *Uttar Pradesh* state, site of the largest *Kumbha Mela* festival.

Arjuna. One of the *Pandavas,* heroes of the *Mahabharata* epic. In the section of the epic known as the *Bhagavad Gita,* Lord *Krishna* appears to Arjuna and advises him as he is about to go into battle.

Aryans. An Indo-European-speaking people who invaded India around 1400 B.C. and eventually merged with the non-Aryan populace. The *Vedic Period* began with that invasion.

Asceticism. Self-denial for purposes of spiritual discipline.

Asramas. The four formal stages of life development: the phases of student, householder, retiree, and spiritual pilgrim. Asramas may only be entered into by the twice-born upper *castes.*

Asura. A demon; an enemy of the gods.

Atman. Soul or inner self. Atman can refer either to the individual soul or to the soul of the Universal Reality (*Brahman*).

Avarna. Without *caste;* those who are outside society, such as the *panchamas.*

Avatara. Incarnation, manifestation, or descent of a god; particularly a manifestation of the god *Vishnu* when he descends to earth in times of crisis.

Ayodhya. One of the holy cities of Hinduism. Ayodhya was the capital of King *Rama,* hero of the *Ramayana* epic.

Banaras. A city of northern India in southeastern *Uttar Pradesh* state.

Bengal. A region in the eastern part of the Indian subcontinent around the delta of the *Ganges* and the Brahmaputra rivers.

Bhagavad Gita, The (lit. "Song of the Blessed Lord"). The section of the *Mahabharata* epic which tells of *Arjuna*'s encounter with Lord *Krishna.* The Bhagavad Gita is the most famous Scripture of Hinduism.

Bhaja Govindam. A hymn written by *Shankara,* an Indian philosopher.

Bhakti (lit. "devotion"). The expression of an individual's faith in, and love of, a god.

Bharata. The legendary emperor from whom India took its traditional name of "Bharat." See also *Bharata Varsha.*

Bharata Natya (lit. "Dance of India"). The most widely known form of India's classical dance.

Bharata Varsha (lit. "Bharata's Land"). India; the land of the legendary emperor *Bharata.*

Bhavani. A manifestation of the goddess *Kali,* especially revered by the *Thugges.*

Brahma. The creator-god of the *Rig Veda.* Brahma is the first god in the Hindu Triad of gods: Brahma the creator, *Vishnu* the preserver, and *Shiva* the destroyer.

Brahman. In Hindu philosophy, the Ultimate Reality, the Universal Self, the Universal Essence.

Brahman-Atman. The unity of the innermost self (*Atman*) with the Universal Self (*Brahman*).

Brahmanism. Early Hinduism; orthodox Hinduism; that of the *Brahmins,* which observes the ancient sacrifices and family ceremonies of Hindu Scriptures.

Brahmans. See *Brahmins.*

Brahmins (also spelled "Brahmans"). Members of the highest *varna,* or occupational grouping, in the *caste* system. Brahmins are priests and teachers.

Brhadaranyaka Upanishad. One of the "forest treatises"—discussions which served as a link between the Brahamanas (treatises explaining the meaning of the *Vedas*) and the *Upanishads.*

Buddhism. The religion which developed from the monastic community established by Guatama Buddha in the sixth century B.C. Buddhism later spread throughout East and Southeast Asia, while it almost disappeared from India.

Calvinism. A Christian religious movement originating in the sixteenth century in Switzerland. Calvinists believed in simplicity of worship and opposed the ornate rituals and dress of other branches of Christianity.

Canarese. Pertaining to a people of *Mysore* who spoke Kannada, the major Dravidian language of that state.

Candalas. See *Chandalas.*

Caste. The hereditary social system of India in which members must follow severe restrictions and rules in matters such as occupations, marriage, and social conduct. The traditional castes are *Brahmin, Kshatriya, Vaishya,* and *Shudra.*

Ceylon. Former name of Sri Lanka, an island republic off the southeastern coast of India.

Chandalas (also spelled "Candalas"). Traditionally, members of non-*Aryan* tribes in India who were considered to be outside the Hindu social system; today, "untouchables"—those who, though Hindu, are considered unclean and outside the *caste* system.

Christianity. The religion that teaches God is the creator and sustainer of the universe and Jesus Christ is its Lord and savior.

Commensality. The practice of habitually eating together. In Hinduism, the restriction against eating with members of a lower *caste.*

Desire, Path of. See *Path of Desire.*

Dharma. Duty; right action according to law and duty.

Dharma Shastra. Books of proper *dharma;* sacred lawbooks; rules of conduct.

Dipvali. See *Divali.*

Divali (also spelled "Dipvali"). The Festival of Lights: an important five-day Hindu celebration in October when many lights are lit to commemorate the return of King *Rama,* hero of the *Ramayana,* to his people.

Durga. A manifestation of *Parvati* (wife of the god *Shiva*) who is particularly honored in *Bengal.*

Endogamous. Relating to marriage within one's own *caste* as required by social custom.

Excommunication. Exclusion from the rights and privileges of membership within a group, especially a religious body.

Ganapati. See *Ganesha.*

Ganapati Puja. The most important festival in *Maharashtra,* held in honor of the god *Ganesha* (or Ganapati).

Ganesha (also spelled "Ganapati"). The elephant-headed god, son of *Shiva,* known as "the remover of all obstacles." He is especially popular in *Maharashtra* where a special festival, the *Ganapati Puja,* is held in his honor.

Ganges River. The great holy river in India which rises out of the Himalayas and flows eastward across the great plain of northern India.

Gita. See *Bhagavad Gita, The.*

Goala. A member of a subcaste of milkmen.

Gujarat. A state in western India near the Gulf of Cambray.

Guru. A religious teacher and spiritual guide.

Hamsa. The *caste* that embraced all individuals in the Hindu mythological *Krita-yuga,* or "first age."

Hanuman. The monkey god who helped *Rama* rescue *Sita* in the *Ramayana* epic.

Hare Krishna. A modern Hindu movement, based on devotion to the god *Krishna,* which has become popular in North America.

Hedonists. Those who believe that the pursuit of pleasure and sensual satisfaction is the chief goal of life.

Holi. A popular spring festival associated with the god *Kama,* characterized by mirth, pranks, and practical jokes.

Indus Valley Civilization. The earliest major civilization in India, which flourished about 2000 B.C. Its base was mainly agricultural, with important urban centers at Mohenjo-Daro and Harappa along the Indus River in the northwestern section of the subcontinent.

Islam. The religion founded by Muhammad in present-day Saudi Arabia in the early seventh century which teaches that there is but one God, Allah, and Muhammad is his prophet.

Iyenar. The invisible watchman who keeps evil away; a local spirit honored in parts of southern India.

Jainism. The religion founded in the sixth century B.C. by Mahavira, whose central doctrines are the perfectability of mankind and a reverence for all forms of life.

Jumna River. A sacred river in *Uttar Pradesh* state which flows south from the Himalayas into the *Ganges River.*

Kala. Time.

Kalakshetra. A dance school in the city of *Madras.*

Kali. A fierce goddess who is one of the manifestations of *Parvati* (wife of the god *Shiva*) and is especially popular in *Bengal.*

Kalidasa. An Indian poet-dramatist of around the fifth century B.C. who is particularly renowned for his play "Shakuntala," adapted from an episode in the *Mahabharata.*

Kama. The god of love, particularly associated with the festival of *Holi.*

Kanya Kumari (lit. "the youthful virgin"). The goddess from whom the present town of Kanniyakumari derived its name. This town is on Cape Comorin, the southernmost point of India, and is noted for its temple and Gandhi memorial.

Karma (lit. "the fruit of one's actions"). The individual's fate in this life as a result of good or bad deeds performed in previous lives; the law of moral causation.

Karma Yoga. A path to salvation consisting of doing good deeds and performing one's duty, or *dharma.*

Kartik (also spelled "Kartlika"). One of the months of the Hindu lunar calendar, approximating our October-November.

Kathakali. An ancient dance form of southwestern India, performed by young boys and men, portraying incidents from the *Ramayana* and the *Mahabharata* epics.

Kauravas, The. Cousins of the *Pandavas*, with whom they warred. The story of that great war is the subject of the *Mahabharata*.

Kerala. A state in southwestern India which borders the Arabian Sea.

Koran (also spelled "Qur'an"). The sacred Scriptures of *Islam*.

Krishna. The best-known and most widely worshipped manifestation of the god *Vishnu*. In the *Bhagavad Gita,* he is the friend and advisor of *Arjuna*.

Krita-yuga. The "first age" of Hinduism, a period of bliss when all individuals belonged to the same *caste*.

Kshatriyas. Members of the second *varna*, or occupational grouping, in the *caste* system. Kshatriyas were traditionally warriors and rulers.

Kubera. The god of wealth.

Kumbha. The constellation of Aquarius, from which the festival of *Kumbha Mela* derives part of its name.

Kumbha Mela. An important festival, held once every twelve years, during which millions of Hindus bathe at the same time in the *Ganges River*. The festival is held in four different cities simultaneously, the one at *Allahabad* being the largest.

Kunti. In the *Mahabharata*, an Indian princess and mother of *Arjuna*.

Kusa. An Indian grass used in Hindu ceremonies.

Lakshmi. Wife of the god *Vishnu* and goddess of good fortune and beauty.

Lingam. A phallic symbol closely associated with the god *Shiva*.

Madras. Port city and capital of *Tamil Nadu* state.

Mahabali. Mythical ruler of *Kerala* who was sent to the underworld by *Vishnu*. He is allowed to return to earth each year for the *Onam* festival, held in his honor.

Mahabharata, The. One of the two great epics of India. (The other is the *Ramayana*.) The Mahabharata is the story of the great war between the *Pandava* brothers and their cousins, the *Kauravas*. It includes the *Bhagavad Gita*.

Maharashtra. A state in western India.

Mandala. A paper or silk square or rectangular representation of the universe used for purposes of meditation; a mystical diagram.

Mantra. Sacred verse from the ancient Scriptures, believed to have been revealed to a seer and to have magical effects if repeated silently or aloud.

Manu. The best known of the ancient lawgivers of India, usually credited with defining the *caste* system.

Mariamma. Goddess of smallpox.

Maya. Illusion; phenomena that hide the unity of Absolute Being.

Mesha. One of the months of the Hindu lunar calendar; the constellation Aries, from which the festival of *Kumbha Mela* derives part of its name.

Mlechchhas. Foreigners, or those "barbarians" who have no place in the Hindu social system.

Moksha (lit. "release"). The final liberation from *samsara,* the cycle of continuous rebirth, and the ultimate salvation in Hinduism.

Mukti. Variant of *moksha.*

Muslim. Relating to the religion of *Islam;* a follower of Islam.

Mysore. A state in southwestern India.

Nivid. A formula; a prescribed set of words used in a rite or ceremony.

Om. A sacred syllable symbolizing the Absolute; the most sacred *mantra* from the *Vedas.*

Onam. A festival in *Kerala* during which the annual return of the mythological king *Mahabali* takes place.

Orthodoxy (lit. "proper or right glory"). In keeping with traditional religious practices.

Panchamas. The "fifth *caste*" of the Hindu social order—outcastes, untouchables, depressed peoples, foreigners, and many others who have no place in the Hindu social system.

Panchatantra (lit. "five parts"). A collection of animal stories or fables containing morals.

Pandavas, The. Cousins of the *Kauravas,* with whom they warred. The story of that great war is the subject of the *Mahabharata,* one section of which—the *Bhagavad Gita*—recounts Lord *Krishna*'s advice to the Pandava hero, *Arjuna.*

Panini. A *Sanskrit* grammarian who lived about 300 B.C.

Parvati. Wife of the god *Shiva,* among whose manifestations are *Durga* and *Kali.*

Patanjali. An ancient Hindu philosopher and author of the *Yogasutra,* which sets forth the yoga systems.

Path of Desire. The striving toward the goals of pleasure and success, considered less fulfilling than the *Path of Renunciation.*

Path of Renunciation. The striving toward the goals of duty and liberation from worldly concerns.

Prasada. The offering brought back from a temple which a Hindu shares with friends.

Puja (lit. "worship"). Adoration or worship of any god or deity, especially in a section or room in a home or temple containing images of and offerings to the gods.

Pundits. Scholars; learned men or teachers.

Puritanism. An English Calvinist religion whose members believed in strict, unceremonial worship and attempted to "purify" the Church of England.

Purusha-Sukta. One of the *Rig Veda* hymns, which describes *caste* as having been divinely created.

Radha. According to legend, a young girl whom the god *Vishnu* fell in love with when he came to earth as *Krishna,* the "divine cowherd."

Raga. A series of notes creating a melody in Indian music.

Rama. The hero of the *Ramayana,* who was later considered to be an *avatara* or incarnation of the god *Vishnu.*

Ramakrishna. One of the best known of the Hindu mystics and teachers, born in *Bengal* in 1836 and died in 1886 after a holy life of devotion to *Rama* and *Krishna.*

Ramayana. One of the two great epics of India. (The other is the *Mahabharata.*) The Ramayana is the story of *Rama*'s quest for his abducted wife *Sita* and the regaining of his throne in *Ayodhya.*

Ravana. The demon who kidnapped *Rama*'s wife *Sita* in the *Ramayana* epic.

Renunciation, Path of. See *Path of Renunciation.*

Rig Veda, The. A hymnbook dating back to about 1500 B.C., considered to be the oldest Scriptures of Hinduism.

Rites of Passage. Ceremonies performed at important periods of change in life, such as birth, onset of puberty, marriage, and death.

Samsara. The constant change of the world; the flow of reality in which souls are continually dying and being reborn; broadly, reincarnation.

Sandhya Namaskaram. The evening prayer in a Hindu household.

Sankara. See *Shankara.*

Sanskrit. The ancient and classical language of India, now used only by scholars.

Sarasvati. Wife of *Brahma* the creator; goddess of learning and patroness of artists and scientists.

Sarasvati Puja. A festival of honor of the goddess of learning, *Sarasvati.*

Sari. The standard dress of Indian women, composed of six yards of cloth wrapped in a prescribed way around the body.

Shaivite. A worshipper of the god *Shiva.*

Shaktis (lit. "powers"). Goddesses or the wives of gods.

Shankara (also spelled "Sankara"). An eighth- to ninth-century philosopher of India who founded the school of thought known as "Advaita Vedanta," based on the teachings of the *Upanishads.*

Shiva (also spelled "Siva"). The destroyer god of the *Rig Veda.* Shiva is the third god in the Hindu Triad: *Brahma* the creator, *Vishnu* the preserver, and Shiva the destroyer.

Shruti (lit. "that which is heard"). The most sacred Scriptures of Hinduism—the *Vedas*, the *Upanishads*, and so forth.

Shudras. Members of the fourth *varna*, or occupational grouping, in the *caste* system. Shudras are the servants of the higher castes.

Sikhism. A militant, monotheistic religion of northern India that originated around 1500 and incorporates elements of both Hinduism and *Islam*.

Sita. The heroine of the *Ramayana* epic, wife of *Rama*.

Siva. See *Shiva*.

Smriti (lit. "that which is remembered"). A collection of Hindu Scriptures less holy than the *shruti*—the *Mahabharata* and the *Ramayana* epics, for instance.

Sonar. A member of a subcaste of goldsmiths.

Sraddha. A memorial ceremony for one's dead ancestors.

Sutar. A member of a subcaste of carpenters.

Sutra. A brief rule or statement summarizing a doctrine or teaching.

Swami. A respectful form of address to a Hindu ascetic or religious teacher, especially one who has renounced the world.

Tamil Nadu. A state in southeastern India which borders the Bay of Bengal.

Teli. A member of a subcaste of oil merchants.

Thirukkural. An ancient text on philosophy and morals from southern India.

Thugges. A semireligious group of zealots dedicated to the goddess *Kali* who practiced ritualistic murder. This group was finally wiped out in the late nineteenth century.

Upanishads. The final section of the Indian Vedic Scriptures, written about the fifth century B.C., which contain some of the earliest philosophical thought of India, including details of Hindu beliefs about the universe and Ultimate Reality.

Uttar Pradesh. A state in northern India on the borders of Tibet and Nepal.

Vaishyas. Members of the third *varna*, or occupational grouping, in the *caste* system. Vaishyas are the business people and merchants.

Vaisnavite. A worshipper of the god *Vishnu*.

Vamana. A dwarf in the *Mahabali* story who was one of the *avataras* of the god *Vishnu*.

Varna. A category in the *caste* system which identifies large occupational groupings. At one time "varna" referred to skin color.

Vedas, The. The oldest and primary Scriptures of Hinduism. See *Rig Veda, The*.

Vedic Period, The. The years from about 1400 to 500 B.C., beginning with the arrival of the *Aryans* in India.

Vina. A stringed musical instrument.

Vishau. The god of preservation.

Vishnu. The preserver god of the *Rig Veda.* Vishnu is the second god in the Hindu Triad: *Brahma* the creator, Vishnu the preserver, and *Shiva* the destroyer.

Yama. The god of death.

Yoga (lit. "yoke"). A discipline or path by which an individual seeks release from the world; a system of exercises designed to bring about mental and physical well-being.

Yogasutra. An ancient philosophical text written by *Patanjali.*